Our Savior's Cries from the Cross

Charles Haddon Spurgeon

Our Savior's Cries from the Cross

© 2018 by Cross-Points Books

ISBN: 9781982969011

All Scripture is taken from the *King James Version*.

Material sourced from The Metropolitan Tabernacle Pulpit Sermons

CONTENTS

Series Introduction

Foreword

1	THE FIRST CRY FROM THE CROSS	1
2	WITNESSING AT THE CROSS	25
3	THE SADDEST CRY FROM THE CROSS	45
4	THE SHORTEST OF THE CRIES	65
5	IT IS FINISHED!	90
6	OUR LORD'S LAST CRY FROM THE CROSS	115

About the Author

Ministries We Love

SERIES INTRODUCTION

The Best of Charles Spurgeon series brings the best sermons of Charles Haddon Spurgeon and makes them accessible in topical volumes.

Available Titles:

- Gospel Hope for Anxious Hearts: Trading Fear and Worry for the Peace of God
- Encouraged to Pray: Classic Sermons on Prayer
- Lessons from the Apostle Paul's Prayers
- Our Savior's Cries from the Cross
- Knowing the Holy Spirit: Ten Classic Sermons
- Walking in the Power of the Holy Spirit: Ten Classic Sermons
- O Death, Where Is Your Sting? Classic Sermons on Dying in Christ and Our Heavenly Hope
- God's Purpose for Your Suffering

Visit Cross-Points.org/bestof to learn more or to explore additional titles.

FOREWORD

The words of a dying person are often dramatic and insightful, serving as a window into their soul.

The importance of the dying words of Jesus Christ are only amplified when realizing how all of history led to the cross and how the cross changed everything to follow.

Our Savior's Cries from the Cross shares sermons by Charles Spurgeon on six of Christ's cries from the cross[1]. As you open this volume, our prayer is that your heart would be broken and warmed; broken by your sin that nailed Christ to the cross, and warmed by knowing that "God commendeth his love toward us, in that, while we were yet sinners, Christ died for us" (Romans 5:8).

Let the Prince of Preachers bring you to the foot of the cross to behold the glory of our Savior.

The Cross-Points Publishing Team, May 2018

[1] Spurgeon never preached on John 19:26–27.

1
THE FIRST CRY FROM THE CROSS

"Then said Jesus, Father, forgive them; for they know not what they do."

—*Luke 23:34*

OUR Lord was at that moment enduring the first pains of crucifixion; the executioners had just then driven the nails through his hands and feet. He must have been, moreover, greatly depressed, and brought into a condition of extreme weakness by the agony of the night in Gethsemane, and by the scourgings and cruel mockings which he had endured all through the morning, from Caiaphas, Pilate, Herod, and the Prætorian guards. Yet neither the weakness of the past, nor the pain of the present, could prevent him from continuing in prayer. The Lamb of God was silent to men, but he was not silent to God. Dumb as a sheep before her shearers, he had not a word to say in his own defence to man, but he continues in his heart crying unto his Father, and no pain and no weakness can silence his holy supplications. Beloved, what an example our Lord herein presents to us! Let us continue in prayer so long as our heart beats; let no excess of suffering drive us away from the throne of grace, but rather let it drive us closer to it.

> "Long as they live should Christians pray,
> For only while they pray they live."

To cease from prayer is to renounce the consolations which our case requires. Under all distractions of spirit, and overwhelmings of heart, great God, help us still to pray, and never from the mercy-seat may our footsteps be driven by despair. Our blessed Redeemer persevered in prayer even when the cruel iron rent his tender nerves, and blow after blow of the hammer jarred his whole frame with anguish; and this perseverance may be accounted for by the fact that he was so in the habit of prayer that he could not cease from it; he had acquired a mighty velocity of intercession which forbade him to pause. Those long nights upon the cold mountain side, those many days which had been spent in solitude, those perpetual ejaculations which he was wont to dart up to heaven, all these had formed in him a habit so powerful, that the severest torments could not stay its force. Yet it was more than habit. Our Lord was baptised in the spirit of prayer; he lived in it, it lived in him, it had come to be an element of his nature. He was like that precious spice, which, being bruised, doth not cease to give forth its perfume, but rather yieldeth it all the more abundantly because of the blows of the pestle, its fragrance being no outward and superficial quality, but an inward virtue essential to its nature, which the pounding in the mortar did but fetch from it, causing it to reveal its secret soul of sweetness. So Jesus prays, even as a bundle of myrrh gives forth its smell, or as birds sing because they cannot do otherwise. Prayer enwrapped his very soul as with a garment, and his heart went forth in such array. I repeat it, let this be our example—never, under any circumstances, however severe the trial, or depressing the difficulty, let us cease from prayer.

Observe, further, that our Lord, in the prayer before us, remains in the vigour of faith as to his Sonship. The extreme trial to which he now submitted himself could not prevent his holding fast his Sonship. His prayer begins, "Father." It was not without meaning that he taught us when we pray to say, "Our Father," for our prevalence in prayer will much depend upon our confidence in our relationship to God. Under great losses and crosses, one is apt to think that God is not dealing with us as a father with a child, but rather as a severe judge with a condemned criminal; but the cry of Christ, when he is brought to an extremity which we shall never reach, betrays no faltering in the spirit of sonship. In Gethsemane, when the bloody sweat fell fast upon the ground, his bitterest cry commenced with, "My Father," asking that if it were possible the cup of gall might pass from him; he pleaded with the Lord as his Father, even as he over and over again had called him on that dark and doleful night. Here, again, in this, the first of his seven expiring cries, it is "Father." O that the Spirit that makes us cry, "Abba, Father," may never cease his operations! May we never be brought into spiritual bondage by the suggestion, "If thou be the Son of God;" or if the tempter should so assail us, may we triumph as Jesus did in the hungry wilderness. May the Spirit which crieth, "Abba, Father," repel each unbelieving fear. When we are chastened, as we must be (for what son is there whom his father chasteneth not?) may we be in loving subjection to the Father of our spirits, and live; but never may we become captives to the spirit of bondage, so as to doubt the love of our gracious Father, or our share in his adoption.

More remarkable, however, is the fact that our Lord's prayer to his Father was not for himself. He continued on the cross to pray for himself, it is true, and his lamentable cry, "My God, my God, why hast thou forsaken me?" shows the personality of his prayer; but the first of the seven great cries on the cross has scarcely even an indirect reference to himself. It is, "Father, forgive them." The petition is altogether for others, and though there is an allusion to the cruelties which they were exercising upon himself, yet it is remote; and you will observe, he does not say, "I forgive them"—that is taken for granted—he seems to lose sight of the fact that they were doing any wrong to himself, it is the wrong which they were doing to the Father that is on his mind, the insult which they are paying to the Father, in the person of the Son; he thinks not of himself at all. The cry, "Father, forgive them," is altogether unselfish. He himself is, in the prayer, as though he were not; so complete is his self-annihilation, that he loses sight of himself and his woes. My brethren, if there had ever been a time in the life of the Son of man when he might have rigidly confined his prayer to himself, without any one cavilling thereat, surely it was when he was beginning his death throes. We could not marvel, if any man here were fastened to the stake, or fixed to a cross, if his first, and even his last and all his prayers, were for support under so arduous a trial. But see, the Lord Jesus began his prayer by pleading for others. See ye not what a great heart is here revealed! What a soul of compassion was in the Crucified! How Godlike, how divine! Was there ever such a one before him, who, even in the very pangs of death, offers as his first prayer an intercession for others? Let this unselfish spirit be in you also, my brethren. Look not every man upon his own things, but every man also on the things of others. Love your neighbours as yourselves, and as Christ has set before you this paragon of unselfishness, seek to follow him, treading in his steps.

There is, however, a crowning jewel in this diadem of glorious love. The Sun of Righteousness sets upon Calvary in a wondrous splendour; but amongst the bright colours which glorify his departure, there is this one—the prayer was not alone for others, but it was for his cruellest enemies. His enemies, did I say, there is more than that to be considered. It was not a prayer for enemies who had done him an ill deed years before, but for those who were there and then murdering him. Not in cold blood did the Saviour pray, after he had forgotten the injury, and could the more easily forgive it, but while the first red drops of blood were spurting on the hands which drove the nails; while yet the hammer was bestained with crimson gore, his blessed mouth poured out the fresh warm prayer, "Father, forgive them, for they know not what they do." I say, not that that prayer was confined to his immediate executioners. I believe that it was a far-reaching prayer, which included Scribes and Pharisees, Pilate and Herod, Jews and Gentiles—yea, the whole human race in a certain sense, since we were all concerned in that murder; but certainly the immediate persons, upon whom that prayer was poured like precious nard, were those who there and then were committing the brutal act of fastening him to the accursed tree. How sublime is this prayer if viewed in such a light! It stands alone upon a mount of solitary glory. No other had been prayed like it before. It is true, Abraham, and Moses, and the prophets had prayed for the wicked; but not for wicked men who had pierced their hands and feet. It is true, that Christians have since that day offered the same prayer, even as Stephen cried, "Lay not this sin to their charge;" and many a martyr has made his last words at the stake words of pitying intercession for his persecutors; but you know where they learnt this, let me ask you where did he learn it? Was not Jesus the divine original? He learnt it nowhere; it leaped up from his own Godlike nature. A compassion peculiar to himself dictated this originality of prayer; the inward royalty of his love suggested to him so memorable an intercession, which may serve us for a pattern, but of which no pattern had existed before. I feel as though I could better kneel before my Lord's cross at this moment than stand in this pulpit to talk to you. I want to adore him; I worship him in heart for that prayer; if I knew nothing else of him but this one prayer, I must adore him, for that one matchless plea for mercy convinces me most overwhelmingly of the deity of him who offered it, and fills my heart with reverent affection.

Thus have I introduced to you our Lord's first vocal prayer upon the cross. I shall now, if we are helped by God's Holy Spirit, make some use of it. First, we shall view it as illustrative of our Saviour's intercession; secondly, we shall regard the text as instructive of the church's work; thirdly, we shall consider it as suggestive to the, unconverted.

I. First, my dear brethren, let us look at this very wonderful text as ILLUSTRATIVE OF OUR LORD'S INTERCESSION.

He prayed for his enemies then, he is praying for his enemies now; the past on the cross was an earnest of the present on the throne. He is in a higher place, and in a nobler condition, but his occupation is the same; he continues still before the eternal throne to present pleas on the behalf of guilty men, crying, "Father, O forgive them." All his intercession is in a measure like the intercession on Calvary, and Calvary's cries may help us to guess the character of the whole of his intercession above.

The first point in which we may see the character of his intercession is this—it is most gracious. Those for whom our Lord prayed, according to the text, did not deserve his prayer. They had done nothing which could call forth from him a benediction as a reward for their endeavours in his service; on the contrary, they were most undeserving persons, who had conspired to put him to death. They had crucified him, crucified him wantonly and malignantly; they were even then taking away his innocent life. His clients were persons who, so far from being meritorious, were utterly undeserving of a single good wish from the Saviour's heart. They certainly never asked him to pray for them—it was the last thought in their minds to say, "Intercede for us, thou dying King! Offer petitions on our behalf, thou Son of God!" I will venture to believe the prayer itself, when they heard it, was either disregarded, and passed over with contemptuous indifference, or perhaps it was caught at as a theme for jest. I admit that it seems to be too severe upon humanity to suppose it possible that such a prayer could have been the theme for laughter, and yet there were other things enacted around the cross which were quite as brutal, and I can imagine that this also might have happened. Yet our Saviour prayed for persons who did not deserve the prayer, but, on the contrary, merited a curse—persons who did not ask for the prayer, and even scoffed at it when they heard it. Even so in heaven there stands the great High Priest, who pleads for guilty men—for guilty men, my hearers. There are none on earth that deserve his intercession. He pleads for none on the supposition that they do deserve it. He stands there to plead as the just One on the behalf of the unjust. Not if any man be righteous, but "if any man sin, we have an advocate with the Father." Remember, too, that our great Intercessor pleads for such as never asked him to plead for them. His elect, while yet dead in trespasses and sins, are the objects of his compassionate intercessions, and while they even scoff at his gospel, his heart of love is entreating the favour of heaven on their behalf. See, then, beloved, if such be the truth, how sure you are to speed with God who earnestly ask the Lord Jesus Christ to plead for you. Some of you, with many tears and much earnestness, have been beseeching the Saviour to be your advocate? Will he refuse you? Stands it to reason that he can? He pleads for those that reject his pleadings, much more for you who prize them beyond gold. Remember, my dear hearer, if there be nothing good in you, and if there be everything conceivable that is malignant and bad, yet none of these things can be any barrier to prevent Christ's exercising the office of Intercessor for you. Even for you he will plead. Come, put your case into his hands; for you he will find pleas which you cannot discover for yourselves, and he will put the case to God for you as for his murderers, "Father, forgive them."

A second quality of his intercession is this—its careful spirit. You notice in the prayer, "Father, forgive them, for they know not what they do." Our Saviour did, as it were, look his enemies through and through to find something in them that he could urge in their favour; but he could see nothing until his wisely affectionate eye lit upon their ignorance: "they know not what they do." How carefully he surveyed the circumstances, and the characters of those for whom he importuned! Just so it is with him in heaven. Christ is no careless advocate for his people. He knows your precise condition at this moment, and the exact state of your heart with regard to the temptation through which you are passing; more than that, he foresees the temptation which is awaiting you, and in his intercession he takes note of the future event which his prescient eye beholds. "Satan hath desired to have thee, that he may sift thee as wheat; but I have prayed for thee that thy faith fail not." Oh, the condescending tenderness of our great High Priest! He knows us better than we know ourselves. He understands every secret grief and groaning. You need not trouble yourself about the wording of your prayer, he will put the wording right. And even the understanding as to the exact petition, if you should fail in it, he cannot, for as he knoweth what is the mind of God, so he knoweth what is your mind also. He can spy out some reason for mercy in you which you cannot detect in yourselves, and when it is so dark and cloudy with your soul that you cannot discern a foothold for a plea that you may urge with heaven, the Lord Jesus has the pleas ready framed, and petitions ready drawn up, and he can present them acceptable before the mercy-seat. His intercession, then, you will observe is very gracious, and in the next place it is very thoughtful.

We must next note its earnestness. No one doubts who reads these words, "Father, forgive them, for they know not what they do," that they were heaven-piercing in their fervour. Brethren, you are certain, even without a thought, that Christ was terribly in earnest in that prayer. But there is an argument to prove that. Earnest people are usually witty, and quick of understanding, to discover anything which may serve their turn. If you are pleading for life, and an argument for your being spared be asked of you, I will warrant you that you will think of one when no one else might. Now, Jesus was so in earnest for the salvation of his enemies, that he struck upon an argument for mercy which a less anxious spirit would not have thought of: "They know not what they do." Why, sirs, that was in strictest justice but a scant reason for mercy; and indeed, ignorance, if it be wilful, does not extenuate sin, and yet the ignorance of many who surrounded the cross was a wilful ignorance. They might have known that he was the Lord of glory. Was not Moses plain enough? Had not Esaias been very bold in his speech? Were not the signs and tokens such that one might as well doubt which is the sun in the firmament as the claims of Jesus to be the Messias? Yet, for all that, the Saviour, with marvellous earnestness and consequent dexterity, turns what might not have been a plea into a plea, and puts it thus: "Father, forgive them, for they know not what they do." Oh, how mighty are his pleas in heaven, then, in their earnestness! Do not suppose that he is less quick of understanding there, or less intense in the vehemence of his entreaties. No, my brethren, the heart of Christ still labours with the eternal God. He is no slumbering intercessor, but, for Zion's sake, he doth not hold his peace, and for Jerusalem's sake, he doth not cease, nor will he, till her righteousness go forth as brightness, and her salvation as a lamp that burneth.

It is interesting to note, in the fourth place, that the prayer here offered helps us to judge of his intercession in heaven as to its continuance, perseverance, and perpetuity. As I remarked before, if our Saviour might have paused from intercessory prayer, it was surely when they fastened him to the tree; when they were guilty of direct acts of deadly violence to his divine person, he might then have ceased to present petitions on their behalf. But sin cannot tie the tongue of our interceding Friend. Oh, what comfort is here! You have sinned, believer, you have grieved his Spirit, but you have not stopped that potent tongue which pleads for you. You have been unfruitful, perhaps, my brother, and like the barren tree, you deserve to be cut down; but your want of fruitfulness has not withdrawn the Intercessor from his place. He interposes at this moment, crying, "Spare it yet another year." Sinner, you have provoked God by long rejecting his mercy and going from bad to worse, but neither blasphemy nor unrighteousness, nor infidelity, shall stay the Christ of God from urging the suit of the very chief of sinners. He lives, and while he lives he pleads; and while there is a sinner upon earth to be saved, there shall be an intercessor in heaven to plead for him. These are but fragments of thought, but they will help you, I hope, to realise the intercession of your great High Priest.

Think yet again, this prayer of our Lord on earth is like his prayer in heaven, because of its wisdom. He seeks the best thing, and that which his clients most need, "Father, forgive them." That was the great point in hand; they wanted most of all there and then forgiveness from God. He does not say, "Father, enlighten them, for they know not what they do," for mere enlightenment would but have created torture of conscience and hastened on their hell; but he crieth, "Father, forgive;" and while he used his voice, the precious drops of blood which were then distilling from the nail wounds were pleading too, and God heard, and doubtless did forgive. The first mercy which is needful to guilty sinners is forgiven sin. Christ wisely prays for the boon most wanted. It is so in heaven; he pleads wisely and prudently. Let him alone, he knows what to ask for at the divine hand. Go you to the mercy-seat, and pour out your desires as best you can, but when you have done so always put it thus, "O my Lord Jesus, answer no desire of mine if it be not according to thy judgment; and if in aught that I have asked I have failed to seek for what I want, amend my pleading, for thou art infinitely wiser than I." Oh, it is sweet to have a friend at court to perfect our petitions for us before they come unto the great King. I believe that there is never presented to God anything but a perfect prayer now; I mean, that before the great Father of us all, no prayer of his people ever comes up imperfect; there is nothing left out, and there is nothing to be erased; and this, not because their prayers were originally perfect in themselves, but because the Mediator makes them perfect through his infinite wisdom, and they come up before the mercy-seat moulded according to the mind of God himself, and he is sure to grant such prayers.

Once more, this memorable prayer of our crucified Lord was like to his universal intercession in the matter of its prevalence. Those for whom he prayed were many of them forgiven. Do you remember that he said to his disciples when he bade them preach, "beginning at Jerusalem," and on that day when Peter stood up with the eleven, and charged the people that with wicked hands they had crucified and slain the Saviour, three thousand of these persons who were thus justly accused of his crucifixion became believers in him, and were baptised in his name. That was an answer to Jesus' prayer. The priests were at the bottom of our Lord's murder, they were the most guilty; but it is said, "a great company also of the priests believed." Here was another answer to the prayer. Since all men had their share representatively, Gentiles as well as Jews, in the death of Jesus, the gospel was soon preached to the Jews, and within a short time it was preached to the Gentiles also. Was not this prayer, "Father, forgive them," like a stone cast into a lake, forming at first a narrow circle, and then a wider ring, and soon a larger sphere, until the whole lake is covered with circling waves? Such a prayer as this, cast into the whole world, first created a little ring of Jewish converts and of priests, and then a wider circle of such as were beneath the Roman sway; and to-day its circumference is wide as the globe itself, so that tens of thousands are saved through the prevalence of this one intercession "Father, forgive them." It is certainly so with him in heaven, he never pleads in vain. With bleeding hands, he yet won the day; with feet fastened to the wood, he was yet victorious; forsaken of God and despised of the people, he was yet triumphant in his pleas; how much more so now the tiara is about his brow, his hand grasps the universal sceptre, and his feet are shod with silver sandals, and he is crowned King of kings, and Lord of lords! If tears and cries out of weakness were omnipotent, even more mighty if possible must be that sacred authority which as the risen Priest he claims when he stands before the Father's throne to mention the covenant which the Father made with him. O ye trembling believers, trust him with your concerns! Come hither, ye guilty, and ask him to plead for you. O you that cannot pray, come, ask him to intercede for you. Broken hearts and weary heads, and disconsolate bosoms, come ye to him who into the golden censer will put his merits, and then place your prayers with them, so that they shall come up as the smoke of perfume, even as a fragrant cloud into the nostrils of the Lord God of hosts, who will smell a sweet savour, and accept you and your prayers in the Beloved. We have now opened up more than enough sea-room for your meditations at home this afternoon, and, therefore we leave this first point. We have had an illustration in the prayer of Christ on the cross of what his prayers always are in heaven.

II. Secondly, the text is INSTRUCTIVE OF THE CHURCH'S WORK.

As Christ was, so his church is to be in this world. Christ came into this world not to be ministered unto, but to minister, not to be honoured, but to save others. His church, when she understands her work, will perceive that she is not here to gather to herself wealth or honour, or to seek any temporal aggrandisement and position; she is here unselfishly to live, and if need be, unselfishly to die for the deliverance of the lost sheep, the salvation of lost men. Brethren, Christ's prayer on the cross I told you was altogether an unselfish one. He does not remember himself in it. Such ought to be the church's life-prayer, the church's active interposition on the behalf of sinners. She ought to live never for her ministers or for herself, but ever for the lost sons of men. Imagine you that churches are formed to maintain ministers? Do you conceive that the church exists in this land merely that so much salary may be given to bishops, and deans, and prebends, and curates, and I know not what? My brethren, it were well if the whole thing were abolished if that were its only aim. The aim of the church is not to provide outdoor relief for the younger sons of the nobility; when they have not brains enough to win anyhow else their livelihood, they are stuck into family livings. Churches are not made that men of ready speech may stand up on Sundays and talk, and so win daily bread from their admirers. Nay, there is another end and aim from this. These places of worship are not built that you may sit here comfortably, and hear something that shall make you pass away your Sundays with pleasure. A church in London which does not exist to do good in the slums, and dens, and kennels of the city, is a church that has no reason to justify its longer existing. A church that does not exist to reclaim heathenism, to fight with evil, to destroy error, to put down falsehood, a church that does not exist to take the side of the poor, to denounce injustice and to hold up righteousness, is a church that has no right to be. Not for thyself, O church, dost thou exist, any more than Christ existed for himself. His glory was that he laid aside his glory, and the glory of the church is when she lays aside her respectability and her dignity, and counts it to be her glory to gather together the outcasts, and her highest honour to seek amid the foulest mire the priceless jewels for which Jesus shed his blood. To rescue souls from hell and lead to God, to hope, to heaven, this is her heavenly occupation. O that the church would always feel this! Let her have her bishops and her preachers, and let them be supported, and let everything be done for Christ's sake decently and in order, but let the end be looked to, namely, the conversion of the wandering, the teaching of the ignorant, the help of the poor, the maintenance of the right, the putting down of the wrong, and the upholding at all hazards of the crown and kingdom of our Lord Jesus Christ.

Now the prayer of Christ had a great spirituality of aim. You notice that nothing is sought for these people but that which concerns their souls, "Father, forgive them." And I believe the church will do well when she recollects that she wrestles not with flesh and blood, nor with principalities and powers, but with spiritual wickedness, and that what she has to dispense is not the law and order by which magistrates may be upheld, or tyrannies pulled down, but the spiritual government by which hearts are conquered to Christ, and judgments are brought into subjection to his truth. I believe that the more the church of God strains after, before God, the forgiveness of sinners, and the more she seeks in her life prayer to teach sinners what sin is, and what the blood of Christ is, and what the hell that must follow if sin be not washed out, and what the heaven is which will be ensured to all those who are cleansed from sin, the more she keeps to this the better. Press forward as one man, my brethren, to secure the root of the matter in the forgiveness of sinners. As to all the evils that afflict humanity, by all means take your share in battling with them; let temperance be maintained, let education be supported; let reforms, political and ecclesiastical, be pushed forward as far as you have the time and effort to spare, but the first business of every Christian man and woman is with the hearts and consciences of men as they stand before the everlasting God. O let nothing turn you aside from your divine errand of mercy to undying souls. This is your one business. Tell to sinners that sin will damn them, that Christ alone can take away sin, and make this the one passion of your souls, "Father, forgive them, forgive them! Let them know how to be forgiven. Let them be actually forgiven, and let me never rest except as I am the means of bringing sinners to be forgiven, even the guiltiest of them."

Our Saviour's prayer teaches the church that while her spirit should be unselfish, and her aim should be spiritual, the range of her mission is to be unlimited. Christ prayed for the wicked, what if I say the most wicked of the wicked, that ribald crew that had surrounded his cross! He prayed for the ignorant. Doth he not say, "They know not what they do"? He prayed for his persecutors; the very persons who were most at enmity with him, lay nearest to his heart. Church of God, your mission is not to the respectable few who will gather about your ministers to listen respectfully to their words; your mission is not to the élite and the eclectic, the intelligent who will criticise your words and pass judgment upon every syllable of your teaching; your mission is not to those who treat you kindly, generously, affectionately, not to these I mean alone, though certainly to these as among the rest; but your great errand is to the harlot, to the thief, to the swearer and the drunkard, to the most depraved and debauched. If no one else cares for these, the church always must, and if there be any who are first in her prayers it should be these who alas! are generally last in our thoughts. The ignorant we ought diligently to consider. It is not enough for the preacher that he preaches so that those instructed from their youth up can understand him; he must think of those to whom the commonest phrases of theological truth are as meaningless as the jargon of an unknown tongue; he must preach so as to reach the meanest comprehension; and if the ignorant many come not to hear him, he must use such means as best he may to induce them, nay, compel them to hear the good news. The gospel is meant also for those who persecute religion; it aims its arrows of love against the hearts of its foes. If there be any whom we should first seek to bring to Jesus, it should be just these who are the farthest off and most opposed to the gospel of Christ. "Father, forgive them; if thou dost pardon none besides, yet be pleased to forgive them."

So, too, the church should be earnest as Christ was; and if she be so, she will be quick to notice any ground of hope in those she deals with, quick to observe any plea that she may use with God for their salvation.

She must be hopeful too, and surely no church ever had a more hopeful sphere than the church of this present age. If ignorance be a plea with God, look on the heathen at this day—millions of them never heard Messiah's name. Forgive them, great God, indeed they know not what they do. If ignorance be some ground for hope, there is hope enough in this great city of London, for have we not around us hundreds of thousands to whom the simplest truths of the gospel would be the greatest novelties? Brethren, it is sad to think that this country should still lie under such a pall of ignorance, but the sting of so dread a fact is blunted with hope when we read the Saviour's prayer aright—it helps us to hope while we cry, "Forgive them, for they know not what they do."

It is the church's business to seek after the most fallen and the most ignorant, and to seek them perseveringly. She should never stay her hand from doing good. If the Lord be coming to-morrow, it is no reason why you Christian people should subside into mere talkers and readers, meeting together for mutual comfort, and forgetting the myriads of perishing souls. If it be true that this world is going to pieces in a fortnight, and that Louis Napoleon is the Apocalyptic beast, or if it be not true, I care not a fig, it makes no difference to my duty, and does not change my service. Let my Lord come when he will, while I labour for him I am ready for his appearing. The business of the church is still to watch for the salvation of souls. If she stood gazing, as modern prophets would have her; if she gave up her mission to indulge in speculative interpretations, she might well be afraid of her Lord's coming; but if she goes about her work, and with incessant toil searches out her Lord's precious jewels, she shall not be ashamed when her Bridegroom cometh.

My time has been much too short for so vast a subject as I have undertaken, but I wish I could speak words that were as loud as thunder, with a sense and earnestness as mighty as the lightning. I would fain excite every Christian here, and kindle in him a right idea of what his work is as a part of Christ's church. My brethren, you must not live to yourselves; the accumulation of money, the bringing up of your children, the building of houses, the earning of your daily bread, all this you may do; but there must be a greater object than this if you are to be Christlike, as you should be, since you are bought with Jesus' blood. Begin to live for others, make it apparent unto all men that you are not yourselves the end-all and be-all of your own existence, but that you are spending and being spent, that through the good you do to men God may be glorified, and Christ may see in you his own image and be satisfied.

III. Time fails me, but the last point was to be a word SUGGESTIVE TO THE UNCONVERTED.

Listen attentively to these sentences. I will make them as terse and condensed as possible. Some of you here are not saved. Now, some of you have been very ignorant, and when you sinned you did not know what you did. You knew you were sinners, you knew that, but you did not know the far-reaching guilt of sin. You have not been attending the house of prayer long, you have not read your Bible, you have not Christian parents. Now you are beginning to be anxious about your souls. Remember your ignorance does not excuse you, or else Christ would not say, "Forgive them;" they must be forgiven, even those that know not what they do, hence they are individually guilty; but still that ignorance of yours gives you just a little gleam of hope. The times of your ignorance God winked at, but now commandeth all men everywhere to repent. Bring forth, therefore, fruits meet for repentance. The God whom you have ignorantly forgotten is willing to pardon and ready to forgive. The gospel is just this, trust Jesus Christ who died for the guilty, and you shall be saved. O may God help you to do so this very morning, and you will become new men and new women, a change will take place in you equal to a new birth; you will be new creatures in Christ Jesus.

But ah! my friends, there are some here for whom even Christ himself could not pray this prayer, in the widest sense at any rate, "Father, forgive them; for they know not what they do," for you have known what you did, and every sermon you hear, and especially every impression that is made upon your understanding and conscience by the gospel, adds to your responsibility, and takes away from you the excuse of not knowing what you do. Ah! sirs, you know that there is the world and Christ, and that you cannot have both. You know that there is sin and God, and that you cannot serve both. You know that there are the pleasures of evil and the pleasures of heaven, and that you cannot have both. Oh! in the light which God has given you, may his Spirit also come and help you to choose that which true wisdom would make you choose. Decide to-day for God, for Christ, for heaven. The Lord decide you for his name's sake. Amen.

Delivered on the Lord's-Day Morning, October 24th, 1869.

2
WITNESSING AT THE CROSS

"And one of the malefactors which were hanged railed on him, saying, If thou be Christ, save thyself and us. But the other answering rebuked him, saying, Dost not thou fear God, seeing thou art in the same condemnation? And we indeed justly; for we receive the due reward of our deeds; but this man hath done nothing amiss. And he said unto Jesus, Lord, remember me when thou comest into thy kingdom. And Jesus said unto him, Verily, I say unto thee, to-day shalt thou be with me in paradise."—Luke 23:39–43.

THE dying thief was certainly a very great wonder of grace. He has generally been looked upon from one point of view only, as a sinner called at the eleventh hour, and therefore an instance of special mercy because he was so near to die. Enough has been made of that circumstance by others: to my mind, it is by no means the most important point in the narrative. Had the thief been predestined to come down from the cross and live for half a century longer, his conversion would have been neither more nor less than it was. The work of grace which enabled him to die in peace would, if it had been the Lord's will, have enabled him to live in holiness. We may well admire divine grace when it so speedily makes a man fit for the bliss of heaven, but it is equally to be adored when it makes him ready for the battle of earth. To bear a saved sinner away from all further conflict is great grace; but the power and love of God are, if anything, even more conspicuous when, like a sheep surrounded by wolves, or a spark in the midst of the sea, a believer is enabled to live on in the teeth of an ungodly world and maintain his integrity to the end. Dear friend, whether you die as soon as you are born again, or remain on earth for many years, is comparatively a small matter, and will not materially alter your indebtedness to divine grace. In the one case the great Husbandman will show how he can bring his flowers speedily to perfection; and in the other he will prove how he can preserve them in blooming beauty, despite the frosts and snows of earth's cruel winter: in either case your experience will reveal the same love and power.

There are other things, it seems to me, to be seen in the conversion of the thief, besides the one single matter of his being brought to know the Lord when near to death's door.

Observe the singular fact that our Lord Jesus Christ should die in the company of two malefactors. It was probably planned in order to bring him shame, and it was regarded by those who cried, "Crucify him! crucify him!" as an additional ignominy. Their malice decreed that he should die as a criminal, and with criminals, and in the centre, between two, to show that they thought him the worst of the three; but God in his own way baffled the malice of the foe, and turned it to the triumph and glory of his dear Son; for, had there been no dying thief hanging at his side, then one of the most illustrious trophies of his love would not have been gained, and we should not have been able to sing to his praise:—

> "The dying thief rejoiced to see
>   That fountain in his day;
> And there have I, though vile as he,
>   Washed all my sins away!"

His enemies gave our Lord Jesus an opportunity for still continuing the seeking, as well as the saving of the lost. They found him an occasion for manifesting his conquering grace when they supposed they were heaping scorn upon him. How truly did the prophet in the psalm say, "He that sitteth in the heavens shall laugh, the Lord shall have them in derision"; for that which was meant to increase his misery revealed his majesty. Moreover, though it was intended to add an ingredient of bitterness to his cup, I do not doubt that it supplied him with a draught of comfort. Nothing could so well have cheered the heart of Jesus, and taken off his mind for just an instant from his own bitter pangs, as having an object of pity before him, upon whom he could pour his mercy. The thief's confession of faith and expiring prayer must have been music to his Saviour's ear, the only music which could in any degree delight him amid his terrible agonies. To hear and to answer the prayer, "Lord, remember me when thou comest into thy kingdom," afforded our Lord a precious solace. An angel strengthened him in the garden, but here it was a man, nailed up at his side, who ministered consolation by the indirect, but very effective method of seeking help at his hands.

Furthermore, the long-continued testimony and witness for Christ among men was at that time exceedingly feeble and ready to expire, and the thief's confession maintained it. The apostles, where were they? They had fled. Those disciples who ventured near enough to see the Lord scarcely remained within speaking distance. They were poor confessors of Christ, scarcely worthy of the name. Was the chain of testimony to be broken? Would none declare his sovereign power? No, the Lord will never let that testimony cease, and lo! he raises up a witness where least you would expect it—on the gibbet. One just ready to die bears witness to the Redeemer's innocence and to his assured coming to a kingdom. As many of the boldest testimonies to Christ have come from the stake, so here was one that came from the gibbet, and gained for the witness the honour of being the last testifier to Christ before he died.

Let us always expect, then, dear friends, that God will overrule the machinations of the foes of Christ so as to get honour from them. At all times of the world's history, when things appear to have gone to pieces, and Satan seems to rule the hour, do not let us despair, but be quite sure that, somehow or other, light will come out of darkness, and good out of evil.

We will now come close up to the dying thief, and look, first, at his faith; secondly, at his confession of faith; thirdly, at his prayer of faith; and fourthly, at the answer of his faith. First, then, may the Holy Ghost help us concerning this dying malefactor, to consider:—

I. HIS FAITH.

It was of the operation of the Spirit of God, and there was nothing in his previous character to lead up to it. How came that thief to be a believer in Jesus? You who carefully read the gospels will have noticed that Matthew says (Matt. 27:44), "The thieves also, which were crucified with him, cast the same in his teeth." Mark also says, "They that were crucified with him reviled him." These two evangelists plainly speak of both thieves as reviling our Lord. How are we to understand this? Would it be right to say that those two writers speak in broad terms of the thieves as a class, because one of them so acted, just as we in common conversation speak of a company of persons doing so and so, when, in fact, the whole matter was the deed of one man of the party? Was it a loose way of speaking? I think not: I do not like the look of suppositions of error in the inspired volume. Would it not be more reverent to the Word of God to believe that the thieves did both revile Jesus? May it not be true that, at the first, they both joined in saying, "If thou be the Christ, save thyself and us," but that afterwards one, by a miracle of sovereign grace, was led to a change of mind, and became a believer? Or would this third theory meet the case, that at the first the thief who afterwards became a penitent, having no thought upon the matter, by his silence gave consent to his fellow's reviling so as fairly to come under the charge of being an accomplice therein: but when it gradually dawned upon his mind that he was under error as to this Jesus of Nazareth, it pleased God in infinite mercy to change his mind, so that he became a confessor of the truth, though he had at first silently assented to the blasphemy of his companion? It would be idle to dogmatize, but we will gather this lesson from it—that faith may enter the mind, notwithstanding the sinful state in which the man is found. Grace can transform a reviling thief into a penitent believer.

Neither do we know the outward means which led to this man's conversion. We can only suppose that he was affected by seeing the Lord's patient demeanour, or, perhaps, by hearing that prayer, "Father, forgive them, for they know not what they do." Surely there was enough in the sight of the crucified Lord with the blessing of God's Spirit to turn a heart of stone into flesh. Possibly the inscription over the head of our

Lord may have helped him—"Jesus of Nazareth, the King of the Jews." Being a Jew, he knew something of the Scriptures, and putting all the facts together, may he not have seen in the prophecies a light which gathered around the head of the sufferer, and revealed him as the true Messiah? Possibly the malefactor remembered Isaiah's words, "He is despised and rejected of men; a man of sorrows, and acquainted with grief: and we hid as it were our faces from him; he was despised, and we esteemed him not." Or, perhaps, the saying of David, in the twenty-second Psalm, rushed upon his memory, "They pierced my hands and my feet." Other texts which he had learned in his youth at his mother's knee may have come before his mind, and putting all these together, he may have argued, "It may be. Perhaps it is. It is. It must be. I am sure it is. It is the Messiah, led as a lamb to the slaughter." All this is but our supposition, and it leads me to remark that there is much faith in this world which cometh, "not with observation," but is wrought in men by unknown instrumentalities, and so long as it really exists it matters very little how it entered the heart, for in every case it is the work of the Holy Ghost. The history of faith is of small importance compared with the quality of faith.

We do not know the origin of this man's faith, but we do know that it was amazing faith under the circumstances. I very gravely question whether there was ever greater faith in this world than the faith of this thief; for he, beyond all others, realised the painful and shameful death of the Lord Jesus, and yet believed. We hear of our Lord's dying upon the cross, but we do not realise the circumstances; and, indeed, even if we were to think upon that death very long and intently, we shall never realise the shame, and weakness, and misery which surrounded our Lord as that dying thief did, for he himself was suffering the pangs of crucifixion at the Saviour's side, and therefore to him it was no fiction, but a vivid reality. Before him was the Christ in all his nakedness and ignominy surrounded by the mocking multitude, and dying in pain and weakness, and yet he believed him to be Lord and King. What think you, sirs? Some of you say you find it hard to believe in Jesus, though you know that he is exalted in the highest heavens; but had you seen him on the cross, had you seen his marred countenance and emaciated body, could you then have believed on him, and said, "Lord remember me when thou comest into thy kingdom"? Yes, you could have done so if the Spirit of God had created faith in you like to that of the thief; but it would have been faith of the first order, a jewel of priceless value. As I said before, so say I again, the vivid sympathy of the thief with the shame and suffering of the Lord rendered his faith remarkable in the highest degree.

This man's faith, moreover, was singularly clear and decided. He rolled his whole salvation upon the Lord Jesus and said, "Lord, remember me when thou comest into thy kingdom." He did not offer a single plea fetched from his doings, his present feelings, or his sufferings; but he cast himself upon the generous heart of Christ. "Thou hast a kingdom: thou art coming to it. Lord, remember me when thou comest into it." That was all. I wish that some who have been professors for years had as clear a faith as the thief; but they are too often confused between law and gospel, works and grace, while this poor felon trusted in nothing but the Saviour and his mercy. Blessed be God for clear faith. I do rejoice to see it in such a case as this, so suddenly wrought and yet so perfect—so outspoken, so intelligent, so thoroughly restful.

That word "restful" reminds me of a lovely characteristic of his faith, namely, its deep peace-giving power. There is a world of rest in Jesus, in the thief's prayer, "Lord, remember me when thou comest into thy kingdom." A thought from Christ is all he wanted, and after the Lord said, "To-day shalt thou be with me in paradise," we never read that the petitioner said another word. I did think that, perhaps, he would have said, "Blessed be the name of the Lord for that sweet assurance. Now I can die in peace"; but his gratitude was too deep for words, and his peace so perfect that calm silence seemed most in harmony with it. Silence is the thaw of the soul, though it be the frost of the mouth; and when the soul flows most freely it feels the inadequacy of the narrow channel of the lips for its great waterfloods.

"Come, then, expressive silence, muse his praise."

He asked no alleviation of pain, but in perfect satisfaction died as calmly as saints do in their beds.

This is the kind of faith which we must all have if we would be saved. Whether we know how we come by it or not, it must be a faith which rolls itself upon Christ, and a faith which consequently brings peace to the soul. Do you possess such faith, dear friend? If you do not, remember that you may die on a sudden, and then into Paradise you will never enter. Look well to this, and believe in the Lord Jesus at once. And now in the second place, we are going to look at this man's:—

II. CONFESSION OF FAITH.

He had faith, and he confessed it. He could neither be baptized nor sit at the communion table, nor unite with the church below; he could not do any of those things which are most right and proper on the part of other Christians, but he did the best he could under the circumstances to confess his Lord.

He confessed Christ, first of all, almost of necessity, because a holy indignation made him speak out. He listened for a while to his brother thief, but while he was musing, the fire burned, then spake he with his tongue, for he could no longer bear to hear the innocent sufferer reviled. He said, "Dost not thou fear God, seeing thou art in the same condemnation? And we, indeed, justly; for we receive the due reward of our deeds: but this man hath done nothing amiss." Did this poor thief speak out so bravely, and can some of you silent Christians go up and down the streets, and hear men curse and blaspheme the name of Christ, and not feel stirred in spirit to defend his cause? While men are so loud in their revilings, can you be quiet? The stones you tread on may well cry out against you. If all were Christians, and the world teemed with Jesus' praise, we might, perhaps, afford to be silent; but, amidst abounding superstition and loud-mouthed infidelity, we are bound to show our colours, and avow ourselves on Christ's side. We doubt not that the penitent thief would have owned his Lord apart from the railing of his comrade; but, as it happened, that reviling was the provoking cause. Does no such cause arouse you? Can you play the coward at such a time as this?

Observe next, that he made a confession to an unsympathetic ear. The other thief does not seem to have made any kind of reply to him, but it is feared that he died in sullen unbelief. The believing thief made his confession where he could not expect to gain approbation, yet he made it none the less clearly. How is it that some dear friends who love the Lord have never confessed their faith, even to their Christian brethren? You know how glad we should be to hear of what the Lord has done for you, but yet we have not heard it. There is a mother who would be so happy if she did but know that her boy was saved, or that her girl was converted, and you have refused her that joy by your silence. This poor thief spoke for Jesus to one who did not enter into his religious experience, and you have not even told yours to those who would have communed with you and rewarded you with comfort and instruction. I cannot understand cowardly lovers of Christ. How you manage to smother your love so long I cannot tell. Love is usually like a cough, which speaks for itself, or a candle which must be seen, or a sweet perfume which is its own revealer; how is it that you have been able to conceal the day which has dawned in your hearts? What can be your motive for coming to Jesus by night only? I cannot understand your riddle, and I hope you will explain it away. Do confess Jesus if you love him, for he bids you do it, and says, "He that confesseth me before men, him will I confess before my Father which is in heaven."

Observe well that this poor thief's confession of faith was attended with a confession of sin. Though he was dying a most horrible death by crucifixion, yet he confessed that he was suffering justly. "We indeed justly." He made his confession not only to God, but to men, justifying the law of his country under which he was then suffering. True faith confesses Christ, and, at the same time, confesses its sin. There must be repentance of sin and acknowledgment of it before God if faith is to give proof of its truth. A faith that never had a tear in its eye, or a blush on its cheek, is not the faith of God's elect. He who never felt the burden of sin, never felt the sweetness of being delivered from it. This poor thief is as clear in the avowal of his own guilt as in his witness to the Redeemer's innocence. Reader, could we say the same of you?

The thief's confession of faith was exceedingly honouring to the Lord Jesus Christ. He confessed that Jesus of Nazareth had done nothing amiss, when the crowd around the cross were condemning him with speech and gesture. He honoured Christ by calling him Lord while others mocked him; by believing in his kingdom while he was dying on a cross, and by entreating him to remember him though he was in the agonies of death. Do you say that this was not much? Well, I will make bold to ask many a professor whether he could honestly say that throughout the whole of his life he has done as much to honour Christ as this poor thief did in those few minutes. Some of you certainly have not, for you have never confessed him at all; and others have confessed him in such a formal manner that there was nothing in it. Oh, there have been times when, had you played the man, and said right straight out, in the midst of a ribald crew, "I do believe in him whom you scoff, and I know the sweetness of that dear name, which you trample under foot," you might have been the means of saving many souls; but you were silent, and whispered to yourself that prudence was the better part of valour, and so you allowed the honour of your Master to be trailed in the mire. Oh, had you, my sister, taken your stand in the family—had you said, "You may do what you will, but as for me, I will serve the Lord"—you might have honoured God far more than you have done; for I fear you have been living in a halting, hesitating style, giving way to a great deal which you knew was wrong, not bearing your protest, not rebuking your brother in his iniquity, but studying your own peace and comfort instead of seeking the Redeemer's glory. We have heard people talk about this dying thief as if he never did anything for his Master; but let me ask the Christian church if it has not members in its midst—gray-haired members, too, who have never, through fifty years of profession, borne one such bravely honest and explicit testimony for Christ as this man did while he was agonising on the cross. Remember, the man's hands and feet were tortured, and he himself was suffering from that natural fever which attends upon crucifixion; his spirit must have melted within him with his dying griefs, and yet he was as bold in rebuke, as composed in prayer, and as calm in spirit as if he was suffering nothing, and thus he reflected much glory upon his Lord.

One other point about this man's confession is worthy of notice, namely, that he was evidently anxious to change the mind of his companion. He rebuked him, and he reasoned with him. Dear friends, I must again put a personal question. Are there not many professing Christians who have never manifested a tithe as much anxiety for the souls of others as this thief felt? You have been a church member ten years, but did you ever say as much to your brother as this dying thief said to the one who was hanging near him? Well, you have meant to do so. Yes, but did you ever do it? You reply that you have been very glad to join others in a meeting. I know that, too, and so far so good; but did you ever personally say as much to another as this dying man did to his old companion? I fear that some of you cannot say so. I, for my part, bless and magnify the grace of God which gave this man one of the sweet fruits of the Spirit, namely, holy charity towards the soul of another, so soon after he himself had come to believe in Jesus. May we all of us have it yet more and more! So much for the confession of his faith: now a little, in the third place, about:—

III. HIS PRAYER OF FAITH.

"Lord, remember me when thou comest into thy kingdom." He addressed the dying Saviour as divine. Wonderful faith this, to call him Lord who was "a worm and no man," and was hanging there upon the cross to die. What shall we say of those who, now that he is exalted in the highest heavens, yet refuse to own his deity? This man had a clearer knowledge of Christ than they have. The Lord take the scales from their eyes, and make them to pray to Jesus as divine.

He prayed to him also as having a kingdom. That needed faith, did it not? He saw a dying man in the hands of his foes nailed to a cross, and yet he believed that he would come into a kingdom. He knew that Jesus would die before long, the marks of the death-agony were upon him, and yet he believed that he would come to a kingdom. O glorious faith! Dear friend, dost thou believe in Christ's kingdom? Dost thou believe that he reigns in heaven, and that he will come a second time to rule over all the earth? Dost thou believe in Christ as King of kings and Lord of lords? Then pray to him as such, "Lord, remember me when thou comest into thy kingdom." May God give you the faith which set this thief a-praying in so excellent a fashion.

Observe that his prayer was for a spiritual blessing only. The other thief said, "Save thyself and us": he meant, "Save us from this cross. Deliver us from the death which now threatens us." He sought temporal benefits, but this man asked only to be remembered by Christ in his kingdom. Do your prayers run that way, dear friends? Then I bless the Lord that he has taught you to seek eternal rather than temporal blessings. If a sick man cares more for pardon than for health, it is a good sign. Soul mercies will be prized above all others where faith is in active exercise.

Observe how humbly he prays. He did not ask for a place at Christ's right hand; he did not, in fact, ask the Lord to do anything for him, but only to "remember" him. Yet that "remember" is a great word, and he meant much by it. "Do give a thought to thy poor companion who now confesses his faith in thee. Do in thy glory dart one recollection of thy love upon poor me, and think on me for good." It was a very humble prayer, and all the sweeter for its lowliness. It showed his great faith in Jesus, for he believed that even to be remembered by him would be enough. "Give me but the crumbs that fall from thy table, and they shall suffice me: but a thought, Lord Jesus, but one thought from thy loving mind, and that shall satisfy my soul."

Did not his prayer drip with faith as a honeycomb with honey? It seems to me as if laid a-soak in his faith till it was saturated through and through with it, for he prays so powerfully, albeit SO humbly. Consider what his character had been, and yet he says, "Lord, remember me when thou comest into thy kingdom." Note well that it is a thief—an outcast, a criminal on the gallows-tree who thus prays. He is an outcast by his country's laws, and yet he turns to the King of heaven and asks to be remembered. Bad as he is, he believes that the Lord Jesus will have mercy upon him. Oh, brave faith!

We see how strong that faith was, because he had no invitation so to pray. I do not know that he had ever heard Christ preach. No apostle had said to him, "Come to Christ, and you will find mercy," and yet he came to Jesus. Here comes an uninvited guest in the sweet bravery of holy confidence in Christ's majestic love; he comes boldly and pleads, "Lord, remember me." It was strong faith which thus pleaded. Remember, too, that he was upon the verge of death. He knew that he could not live very long, and probably expected the Roman bone-breaker to give him very soon the final blow; but in the very hour and article of death he cried, "Lord, remember me," with the strong confidence of a mighty faith. Glory be to God who wrought such a faith in such a man as this.

We have done when we have mentioned, in the fourth place:—

IV. THE ANSWER TO HIS FAITH.

We will only say that his faith brought him to paradise. We had a paradise once, and the first Adam lost it. Paradise has been regained by the second Adam, and he has prepared for believers an Eden above, fairer than that first garden of delights below. Faith led the dying thief to be with Christ in paradise, which was best of all "To-day shalt thou be with me in paradise." Whatever the joy of Christ, and the glory of Christ, the thief was there to see it and to share it as soon as Christ himself.

And it brought him paradise that very day. Sometimes a crucified man will be two or three days a-dying; Jesus, therefore, assures him that he shall not have long to suffer, and confirms it with a "verily," which was our Lord's strong word of asseveration, "Verily I say unto thee, to-day shalt thou be with me in paradise." Such a portion will faith win for each of us, not to-day it may be, but one day. If we believe in Jesus Christ, who died for our sins, we shall be with him in the delights and happiness of the spirit-world, and with him in the paradise of everlasting glory. If we commenced to believe at once, and were to die immediately, we should be with Christ at once, as surely as if we had been converted fifty years ago. You cannot tell how short your life will be, but it is well to be ready. A friend was here last Sabbath-day of whom I heard this morning that he was ill, and in another hour that he was dead. It was short work; he was smitten down, and gone at once. That may be the lot of any one of you; and if it should be, you will have no cause whatever to fear it if you now, like the thief, trust yourself wholly in Jesus' hands, crying, "Lord, remember me when thou comest into thy kingdom."

The lesson of our text is not merely that Christ can save in our last extremity, though that is true, but that now at this moment Jesus is able to save us, and that, if saved at all, salvation must be an immediate and complete act, so that, come life or come death, we are perfectly saved. It will not take the Lord long to raise the dead—in a moment, in the twinkling of an eye, the dead shall be raised incorruptible; and the Lord takes no time in regenerating a soul. Dead souls live in an instant when the breath of the Spirit quickens them. Faith brings instantaneous pardon. There is no course of probation to go through, there are no attainments to be sought after, and no protracted efforts to be made in order to be saved. Thou art saved if thou believest in Jesus. The finished work of Christ is thine. Thou art God's beloved, accepted, forgiven, adopted child. Saved thou art, and saved thou shalt be for ever and ever if thou believest.

Instantaneous salvation! Immediate salvation! This the Spirit of God gives to those who trust in Jesus. Thou needest not wait till to-morrow's sun has dawned. Talk not of a more convenient season.

Sitting where thou art, the almighty grace of God can come upon thee and save thee, and this shall be a sign unto thee that Christ is born in thy heart the hope of glory—when thou believest in him as thy pardon, righteousness, and all in all, thou shalt have peace. If thou dost but trust thyself in Jesus' hands thou art a saved soul, and the angels in heaven are singing high praises to God and the Lamb on thine account. Farewell.

Published posthumously on Thursday, July 17, 1913.

3
THE SADDEST CRY FROM THE CROSS

"And about the ninth hour Jesus cried with a loud voice, saying, Eli; Eli, lama sabachthani? that is to say, My God, my God, why hast thou forsaken me?"

—Matthew 27:46

DURING the time that "Moses kept the flock of Jethro, his father-in-law," he "came to the mountain of God, even to Horeb," and there he saw a strange sight,—a bush that burned with fire, and yet was not consumed. Then Moses, apparently constrained by curiosity, was drawing near, in order to examine this phenomenon, when he heard God's voice say to him, "Draw not nigh hither: put off thy shoes from off thy feet, for the place whereon thou standest is holy ground." We also may well feel, as we think of our Lord Jesus in his agony, that the voice of God speaks to us from the cross, and says, "Curiosity,—bold, daring, prying intellect,—draw not nigh hither; put off thy shoes from off thy feet, for the place whereon thou standest is the very Holy of Holies, unto which no man may come except as the Spirit of God shall conduct him thither."

I think I can understand the words, "My God, my God, why hast thou forsaken me?" as they are written by David in the 22nd Psalm; but the same words, "My God, my God, why hast thou forsaken me?" when uttered by Jesus on the cross, I cannot comprehend, so I shall not pretend to be able to explain them. There is no plummet that can fathom this deep; there is no eagle's eye that can penetrate the mystery that surrounds this strange question. I have read that, once upon a time, Martin Luther sat him down in his study to consider this text. Hour after hour, that mighty man of God sat still; and those who waited on him came into the room, again and again, and he was so absorbed in his meditation that they almost thought he was a corpse. He moved neither hand nor foot, and neither ate nor drank; but sat with his eyes wide open, like one in a trance, thinking over these wondrous words, "My God, my God, why hast thou forsaken me?" And when, after many long hours, in which he seemed to be utterly lost to everything that went on around him, he rose from his chair, someone heard him say, "God forsaking God! No man can understand that;" and so he went his way. Though that is hardly the correct expression to use,—I should hesitate to endorse it,—yet I do not marvel that our text presented itself to the mind of Luther in that light. It is said that he looked like a man who had been down a deep mine, and who had come up again to the light. I feel more like one who has not been down the mine, but who has looked into it,—or like one who has been part of the way down, and shuddered as he passed through the murky darkness, but who would not dare to go much lower, for this cry, "Eli, Eli, lama sabachthani?" is a tremendous deep; no man will ever be able to fathom it.

So I am not going to try to explain it; but, first, to utter some thoughts about, it; and then, secondly, to draw some lessons from it. We may find many practical uses for things which are beyond the grasp of our minds, and this saying of our Lord may be of great service to us even though we cannot comprehend it.

I. First, then, let me utter SOME THOUGHTS ABOUT THIS STRANGE QUESTION: "My God, my God, why hast thou forsaken me?"

Jesus was accustomed to address God as his Father. If you turn to his many prayers, you will find him almost invariably—if not invariably—speaking to God as his Father. And, truly, he stands in that relationship both as God and as man. Yet, in this instance, he does not say, "Father;" but "My God, my God." Was it that he had any doubt about his Sonship? Assuredly not; Satan had assailed him in the wilderness with the insinuation, "If thou be the Son of God," but Christ had put him to the rout; and I feel persuaded that Satan had not gained any advantage over him, even on the cross, which could have made him doubt whether he was the Son of God or not.

I think that our Saviour was speaking then as man, and that this is the reason why he cried, "My God, my God," rather than "My Father." I think he must have been speaking as man; as I can scarcely bring my mind to the point of conceiving that God the Son could say to God the Father, "My God, my God." There is such a wonderful blending of the human and the Divine in the person of the Lord Jesus Christ that, though it may not be absolutely accurate to ascribe to the Deity some things in the life of Christ, yet is he so completely God and man that, often, Scripture does speak of things that must belong to the humanity only as if they belonged to the Godhead. For instance, in his charge to the Ephesian elders, the apostle Paul said, "Feed the church of God, which he hath purchased with his own blood;"—an incorrect expression, if judged according to the rule of the logician; but accurate enough according to the Scriptural method of using words in their proper sense. Yet I do think that we must draw a distinction between the Divinity and the humanity here. As the Lord Jesus said, "My God, my God," it was because it was his humanity that was mainly to be considered just then.

And O my brethren, does it not show us what a real man the Christ of God was, that he could be forsaken of his God? We might have supposed that, Christ being Emmanuel,—God with us,—the Godhead and the manhood being indissolubly united in one person, it would have been impossible for him to be forsaken of God. We might also have inferred, for the same reason, that it would have been impossible for him to have been scourged, and spit upon, and especially that it would not have been possible for him to die. Yet all these things were made, not only possible, but also sacredly certain. In order to complete the redemption of his chosen people, it was necessary for him to be both God's well-beloved Son, and to be forsaken of his Father; he could truly say, as his saints also have sometimes had to say, "My God, my God, why hast thou forsaken me?" Persecuted and forsaken believer, behold your Brother in adversity! Behold the One who has gone wherever you may have to go, who has suffered more than you can ever suffer, and who has taken his part in the direst calamity that ever happened to human nature, so that he had to cry out, in the agony of his soul, "My God, my God, why hast thou forsaken me?"

What was this forsaking? We are trying to come a little closer to this burning yet unconsumed bush,—with our shoes off our feet, I hope, all the while;—and in this spirit we ask, "What was this forsaking?" A devout writer says that it was horror at the sight of human misery. He affirms, what is quite true, that our Lord Jesus Christ saw all that man had to suffer because of sin; that he perceived the total sum of the miseries brought by sin upon all the past, present, and future generations of the human race;—and that he must have had a holy horror as he thought of all the woes of man, caused by sin, in this life, and in that which is to come;—and being completely one with man, he spoke in the name of man, and said, "My God, my God, why hast thou forsaken me?" That is all true, yet that explanation will not suffice, my brethren; because our Saviour did not say, "My God, my God, why hast thou forsaken man?" but, "Why hast thou forsaken me?" This forsaking was something personal to himself.

Others have said that it was a dreadful shrinking in his soul on account of human sin. I have read of a child, who had done wrong, and whose father had faithfully rebuked and punished him; but the boy remained callous and sullen. He sat in the same room with his father, yet he refused to confess that he had done wrong. At last, the father, under a sense of his child's great wickedness, burst into tears, and sobbed and sighed. Then the boy came to his father, and asked him why he sorrowed so, and he answered, "Because of my child's hardness of heart." It is true that our Lord Jesus Christ did feel as that father felt; only far more acutely; but our text cannot be fully explained by any such illustration as that; that would be only explaining it away, for Christ did not say, "My God, my God, why has man forsaken thee, and why hast thou so completely left men in their sin?" No; his cry was, "Why hast thou forsaken me?" It was not so much the God of man to whom he appealed, but "My God, my God." It was a personal grief that wrung from him the personal cry, "My God, my God, why hast thou forsaken me?" for this forsaking, by his Father in whom he trusted, related peculiarly to himself.

What was this forsaking? Was it physical weakness? Some of you may know that, when the body is in a low condition, the soul also sinks. Quite involuntarily, unhappiness of mind, depression of spirit, and sorrow of heart will come upon you. You may be without any real reason for grief, and yet may be among the most unhappy of men because, for the time, your body has conquered your soul. But, my brethren and sisters, this explanation is not supposable in the case of Christ, for it was not many moments after this that he shouted, "with a loud voice," his conquering cry, "It is finished," and so passed from the conflict to his coronation. His brave spirit overcame his physical weakness; and though he was "brought into the dust of death," and plunged into the deepest depths of depression of spirit, yet, still, the cry, "My God, my God," which also was uttered "with a loud voice," proves that there was still a considerable amount of mental strength, notwithstanding his physical weakness, so that mere depression of spirit, caused by physical reasons, would not account for this agonizing cry.

And, certainly, my brethren, this cry was not occasioned by unbelief. You know that, sometimes, a child of God, in sore trial, and with many inward struggles, cries out, "My God, my God, why hast thou forsaken me?" when, all the while, the Lord has been remembering the tried soul, and dealing graciously with it. As long ago as Isaiah's day, "Zion said, The Lord hath forsaken me, and my Lord hath forgotten me." But the Lord's reply was, "Can a woman forget her sucking child, that she should not have compassion on the son of her womb? yea, they may forget, yet will I not forget thee. Behold, I have graven thee upon the palms of my hands." Unbelief often makes us talk about God forgetting us when he does nothing of the kind, but our Lord Jesus Christ was a stranger to unbelief. It was impossible for him to cherish any doubt about the faithfulness and lovingkindness of his Father; so his cry did not arise from that cause.

And, another thing, it did not arise from a mistake. I have known believers, in sore trouble, make great blunders concerning what God was doing with them. They have thought that he had forsaken them, for they misinterpreted certain signs, and dealings of God, and they said, "All these things are against us; the hand of God has gone out against us to destroy us." But Christ made no mistake about this matter, for God had forsaken him. It was really so. When he said, "Why hast thou forsaken me?" he spoke infallible truth, and his mind was under no cloud whatsoever. He knew what he was saying, and he was right in what he said, for his Father had forsaken him for the time.

What, then, can this expression mean? Does it mean that God did not love his Son? O beloved, let us, with the utmost detestation, fling away any suspicion of the kind that we may have harboured! God did forsake his Son, but he loved him as much when he forsook him as at any other period. I even venture to say that, if it had been possible for God's love towards his Son to be increased, he would have delighted in him more when he was standing as the suffering Representative of his chosen people than ever he had delighted in him before. We do not indulge, for a single moment, the thought that God was angry with him personally, or looked upon him as unworthy of his love, or regarded him as one upon whom he could not smile, because of anything displeasing in himself; yet the fact remains that God had forsaken him, for Christ was under no mistake about that matter. He rightly felt that his Father had withdrawn the comfortable light of his countenance, that he had, for the time being, lost the sense of his Father's favour,—not the favour itself, but the consciousness of that divine aid and succour which he had formerly enjoyed;—so he felt himself like a man left all alone; and he was not only left all alone by his friends, but also by his God.

Can we at all imagine the state of mind in which our Lord was when he cried, "My God, my God, why hast thou forsaken me?" No; that is not possible, yet I will try to help you to understand it. Can you imagine the misery of a lost soul in hell,—one who is forsaken of God, and who cries, in bitterest agony, "God will never look upon me in mercy, or delight, or favour,"—can you picture that sad state? Well, if you can, you will not, even then, have got anywhere near the position of Christ, because that soul in hell does not want God's favour, and does not seek it, or ask for it. That lost soul is so hardened in sin that it never troubles about whether God would receive it if it repented; the truth is, that it does not want to repent. The misery, that men will suffer in the world to come, will be self-created misery arising out of the fact that they loved sin so much that they brought eternal sorrow upon themselves. It must be an awful thing for a soul, in the next world, to be without God; but, as far as its own consciousness is concerned, it will be so hardened that it will abide without God, yet not realizing all that it has lost because it is itself incapable of knowing the beauty of holiness, and the perfection of the God from whom it is separated for ever. Yet how different was the case of our Lord Jesus Christ when upon the cross! He knew, as no mere man could ever know, what separation from God meant.

Think of a case of another kind. King Saul, when the witch of Endor brought up the spirit of Samuel, said to him, "God is departed from me, and answereth me no more." You recollect the state of mind that he was in when the evil spirit was upon him, and he needed David's harp to charm it away; but at last, even that failed, and I know of no more unhappy character than Saul when God had departed from him. But, somehow, there was not the anguish in the soul of Saul that there would have been if he had ever really known the Lord. I do not think that he ever did really, in his inmost soul, know the Lord. After Samuel anointed him, he was "turned into another man," but he never became a new man; and the sense of God's presence that he had was not, for a moment, comparable to that presence of God which a true saint enjoys, and which Christ ever enjoyed, except when he was on the cross. So, when Saul lost the consciousness of that presence, he did not suffer so great a loss, and, consequently, so great an anguish, as afterwards happened to our Lord.

Coming nearer to our own circumstances, I remind you that there are some of God's people, who do really love him, and who have walked in the light of his countenance, yet, for some reason or other, they have lost the comfortable enjoyment of God's love. If any of you, dear friends, know what that sad experience is, you are getting a faint impression of the meaning of this cry, "My God, my God, why hast thou forsaken me?" Oh, what an anguish it is,—what heart-break,—even to think that one is forsaken of God. I have heard of people dying of broken hearts; but I do believe that the man, who has been made to utter this cry, has gone as near to dying of a broken heart as anyone might well do without actually dying. To be without God, is to be without life; and we, who love him, can say, with Dr. Watts,—

> "My God, my life, my love,
> To thee, to thee I call:
> I cannot live, if thou remove,
> For thou art All-in-all."

But, my dear brethren, you have not got the whole truth yet, for no saint knows the presence of God as Christ knew it. No saint has, to the full, enjoyed the love of God as Christ enjoyed it; and, consequently, if he does lose it, he only seems to lose the moonlight whereas Christ lost the sunlight when, for a time, the face of his Father was withdrawn from him. Only think what must have been the anguish of the Saviour, especially as contrasted with his former enjoyment. Never did any mere human being know so much and enjoy so much of the love of God as Christ had done. He had lived in it, basked in it; there had never been any interruption to it. "I do always those things that please him;" said he, concerning his Father; and his Father twice said, concerning him, "This is my beloved Son, in whom I am well pleased." Now, as our Lord Jesus Christ had enjoyed the love of God to the very full, think what it must have been for him to lose the conscious enjoyment of it. You know that you may go into a room, and blow out the candle, but the blind people will not miss it. They miss the light most who have enjoyed it most; and Christ missed the light of God's countenance most because he had enjoyed it most. Then, reflect upon his intense love to God. Jesus Christ—the man Christ Jesus—loved God with all his heart, and mind, and soul, and strength, as you and I have never yet been able to do. The love of Christ towards his Father was boundless. Well, then, for a frown to be upon his Father's face, or for the light of that Father's face to be taken away from him, must have made it correspondingly dark and terrible to him.

Remember, too, the absolute purity of Christ's nature. In him there was no taint or sin, nor anything approaching to it. Now, holiness delights in God. God is the very sea in which holiness swims,—the air which holiness breathes. Only think, then, of the perfectly Holy One, fully agreed with his Father in everything. finding out that the Father had, for good and sufficient reasons, turned away his face from him. O brother, in proportion as you are holy, the absence of the light of God's countenance will be grief to you; and as Jesus was perfectly holy, it was the utmost anguish to him to have to cry to his Father, "Why hast thou forsaken me?"

After all, beloved, the only solution of the mystery is this, Jesus Christ was forsaken of God because we deserved to be forsaken of God. He was there, on the cross, in our room, and place, and stead; and as the sinner, by reason of his sin, deserves not to enjoy the favour of God, so Jesus Christ, standing in the place of the sinner, and enduring that which would vindicate the justice of God, had to come under the cloud, as the sinner must have come, if Christ had not taken his place. But, then, since he has come under it, let us recollect that he was thus left of God that you and I, who believe in him, might never be left of God. Since he, for a little while, was separated from his Father, we may boldly cry, "Who shall separate us from the love of Christ?" and, with the apostle Paul, we may confidently affirm that nothing in the whole universe "shall be able to separate us from the love of God, which is in Christ Jesus our Lord."

Before I leave this point, let me say that the doctrine of substitution is the key to all the sufferings of Christ. I do not know how many theories have been invented to explain away the death of Christ. The modern doctrine of the apostles of "culture" is that Jesus Christ did something or other, which, in some way or other, was, in some degree or other, connected with our salvation; but it is my firm belief that every theory, concerning the death of Christ, which can only be understood by the highly-cultured, must be false. "That is strong language," says someone. Perhaps it is, but it is true. I am quite sure that the religion of Jesus Christ was never intended for the highly-cultured only, or even for them in particular. Christ's testimony concerning his own ministry was, "The poor have the gospel preached to them;" so, if you bring me a gospel which can only be understood by gentlemen who have passed through Oxford or Cambridge University, I know that it cannot be the gospel of Christ. He meant the good news of salvation to be proclaimed to the poorest of the poor; in fact, the gospel is intended for humanity in general; so, if you cannot make me understand it, or if, when I do understand it, it does not tell me how to deliver its message in such plain language that the poorest man can comprehend it, I tell you, sirs, that your newfangled gospel is a lie, and I will stick to the old one, which a man, only a little above an idiot in intellect, can understand. I cling to the old gospel for this, among many other reasons, that all the modern gospels, that leave out the great central truth of substitution, prevent the message from being of any use to the great mass of mankind. If those other gospels, which are not really gospels, please your taste and fancy, and suit the readers of Quarterly Reviews, and eloquent orators and lecturers, there are the poor people in our streets, and the millions of workingmen, the vast multitudes who cannot comprehend anything that is highly metaphysical; and you cannot convince me that our Lord Jesus Christ sent, as his message to the whole world, a metaphysical mystery that would need volume upon volume before it could even be stated. I am persuaded that he gave us a rough and ready gospel like this, "The Son of man is come to seek and to save that which was lost;" or this, "With his stripes we are healed;" or this, "The chastisement of our peace was upon him;" or this, "He died the Just for the unjust to bring us to God." Do not try to go beyond this gospel, brethren; you will get into the mud if you do. But it is safe standing here; and standing here, I can comprehend how our Lord Jesus took the sinner's place, and passing under the sentence which the sinner deserved, or under a sentence which was tantamount thereto, could cry, "My God, my God, why hast thou forsaken me?—

II. Now, in closing, I am going to draw A FEW LESSONS FROM THIS UTTERANCE OF CHRIST.

The first lesson is, Behold how he loved us! When Christ stood and wept at the grave of Lazarus, the Jews said, "Behold how he loved him!" But on the cross he did not weep, he bled; and he not merely bled, he died; and, before he died, his spirit sank within him, for he was forsaken of his God. Was there ever any other love like this,—that the Prince of life and glory should condescend to this shame and death?

Then, next, brothers and sisters, as he suffered so much for us, let us be ready to suffer anything for his sake. Let us be willing even to lose all the joy of religion, if that would glorify God. I do not know that it would; but I think the spirit of Christ ought to carry us even as far as Moses went, when he pleaded for the guilty nation of Israel, and was willing to have his own name-blotted out of the book of life rather than that God's name should be dishonoured. We have never had to go so far as that, and we never shall; yet let us be willing to part with our last penny, for Christ's name's sake, if he requires it. Let us be willing to lose our reputation. Ah, it is a difficult thing to give that up! Some of us, when we first came into public notice, and found our words picked to pieces, and our character slandered, felt it rather hard. We have got used to it now; but it was very trying at first. But, oh! if one had to be called a devil,—if one had to go through this world, and to be spat upon by every passer-by,—still, if it were endured for Christ's sake, remembering how he was forsaken of God for us, we ought to take up even that cross with thankfulness that we were permitted to bear it.

Another lesson is that, if ever you and I should feel that we are forsaken of God,—if we should get into this state in any way, remember that we are only where Christ has been before us. If ever, in our direst extremity, we should be compelled to cry, "My God, my God, why hast thou forsaken me?" we shall have gone down no deeper than Christ himself went. He knows that feeling, and that state of heart, for he has felt the same. This fact should tend greatly to cheer you. Your deep depression is not a proof of reprobation; that is evident, for Christ himself endured even more. A man may say, "I cannot be a child of God, or else I should not feel as I do." Ah! you do not know what true children of God may feel; strange thoughts pass through their minds in times of storm and doubt. A Puritan preacher was standing by the death-bed of one of his members who had been for thirty years in gloom of soul. The good old minister expected that the man would get peace at last, for he had been an eminent Christian, and had greatly rejoiced in his Saviour; but, for thirty years or more, he had fallen into deep gloom. The minister was trying to speak a word of comfort to him, but the man said, "Ah, sir! but what can you say to a man who is dying, and yet who feels that God has forsaken him?" The pastor replied, "But what became of that Man who died, whom God did really forsake? Where is HE now?" The dying man caught at that, and said, "He is in glory, and I shall be with him; I shall be with him where he is." And so the light came to the dying man who had been so long in the dark; he saw that Christ had been just where he was, and that he should be where Christ was, even at the right hand of the Father. I hope, brothers and sisters, that you will never get down so low as that; but I beseech you, if you ever meet with any others who are there, do not be rough with them. Some strong-minded people are very apt to be hard upon nervous folk, and to say, "They should not get into that state." And we are liable to speak harshly to people who are very depressed in spirit, and to say to them, "Really, you ought to rouse yourself out of such a state." I hope none of you will ever have such an experience of this depression of spirit as I have had; yet I have learnt from it to be very tender with all fellow-sufferers. The Lord have mercy on them, and help them out of the Slough of Despond; for, if he does not, they will sink in deep mire, where there is no standing.

I pray God specially to bless this inference from our text. There is hope for you, brother, or sister, if you are in this condition. Christ came through it, and he will be with you in it; and, after all, you are not forsaken as he was, be you sure of that. With you, the forsaking is only in the apprehension; that is bad enough, but it is not a matter of fact, for "the Lord will not forsake his people," nor cast away even one of those whom he has chosen.

I will tell you what is a much more awful thing even than crying out, "My God, my God, why hast thou forsaken me?" If you are afraid that God has left you, and the sweat stands on your brow in very terror, and if your soul seems to long for death rather than life, in such a state as that, you are not in the worst possible condition. "Why!" you ask, "is there anything worse than that?" Yes, I will tell you what is much worse than that; that is, to be without God, and not to care about it;—to be living, like some whom I am now addressing, without God, and without hope, yet that never concerns them at all. I can pity the agony of the man who cannot bear to be without his God; but, at the same time, I can bless the Lord that he feels such agony as that, for that proves to me that his soul will never perish. But those, whom I look upon with fear and trembling, are the men who make a profession of religion, yet who never have any communion with God, and, all the while, are quite happy about it;—or backsliders, who have gone away from God, and yet seem perfectly at ease. You, worldlings, who are quite satisfied with the things of this world, and have no longings for the world that is to come, I wish you had got as far as to be unhappy; I wish you had got as far as to be in an agony, for that is the road to heavenly joy. It was thus that Christ won it for us, and it is by such a path as this, that many a soul is first led into the experience of his saving power. Brethren, weep not for those of us who sometimes have to cry out in anguish of soul; mourn not for us who are cast down because we cannot live without Christ. You see that our Lord has made us covet the highest blessings; our heads have been so often on his bosom that, if they are not always there, we keep on crying till we get back to that blessed position again. This is a sweet sorrow; may we have more and more of it! But, oh! I pray you, pity those who never ate the bread of heaven,—never drank of the water of life,—never knew the sweetness of the kisses of Christ's mouth,—

and never knew what it was to have a heaven begun below in the enjoyment of fellowship with him. In such cases, your pity is indeed required.

I have finished when I have just said this,—as you come to the table of your Lord, come, brothers and sisters, with this cry of Christ ringing in your ears, to make you love him more than ever; and, as you eat the bread, and drink the wine, do it all out of fervent love to him; and the Lord bless you, for his name's sake! Amen.

Preached on Lord's-day Evening, January 7th, 1877.

4
THE SHORTEST OF THE CRIES

"After this, Jesus knowing that all things were now accomplished, that the scripture might be fulfilled, saith,

'I thirst.'"

—John 19:28

IT was most fitting that every word of our Lord upon the cross should be gathered up and preserved. As not a bone of him shall be broken, so not a word shall be lost. The Holy Spirit took special care that each of the sacred utterances should be fittingly recorded. There were, as you know, seven of those last words, and seven is the number of perfection and fulness; the number which blends the three of the infinite God with the four of complete creation. Our Lord in his death-cries, as in all else, was perfection itself. There is a fulness of meaning in each utterance which no man shall be able fully to bring forth, and when combined they make up a vast deep of thought, which no human line can fathom. Here, as everywhere else, we are constrained to say of our Lord, "Never man spake like this man." Amid all the anguish of his spirit his last words prove him to have remained fully self-possessed, true to his forgiving nature, true to his kingly office, true to his filial relationship, true to his God, true to his love of the written word, true to his glorious work, and true to his faith in his Father.

As these seven sayings were so faithfully recorded, we do not wonder that they have frequently been the subject of devout meditation. Fathers and confessors, preachers and divines have delighted to dwell upon every syllable of these matchless cries. These solemn sentences have shone like the seven golden candlesticks or the seven stars of the Apocalypse, and have lighted multitudes of men to him who spake them. Thoughtful men have drawn a wealth of meaning from them, and in so doing have arranged them into different groups, and placed them under several heads. I cannot give you more than a mere taste of this rich subject, but I have been most struck with two ways of regarding our Lord's last words. First, they teach and confirm many of the doctrines of our holy faith. "Father, forgive them; for they know not what they do" is the first. Here is the forgiveness of sin—free forgiveness in answer to the Saviour's plea. "To-day shalt thou be with me in paradise." Here is the safety of the believer in the hour of his departure, and his instant admission into the presence of his Lord. It is a blow at the fable of purgatory which strikes it to the heart. "Woman, behold thy son!" This very plainly sets forth the true and proper humanity of Christ, who to the end recognised his human relationship to Mary, of whom he was born. Yet his language teaches us not to worship her, for he calls her "woman," but to honour him who in his direst agony thought of her needs and griefs, as he also thinks of all his people, for these are his mother and sister and brother. "Eloi, Eloi, lama sabachthani?" is the fourth cry, and it illustrates the penalty endured by our Substitute when he bore our sins, and so was forsaken of his God. The sharpness of that sentence no exposition can fully disclose to us: it is keen as the very edge and point of the sword which pierced his heart. "I thirst" is the fifth cry, and its utterance teaches us the truth of Scripture, for all things were accomplished, that the Scripture might be fulfilled, and therefore our Lord said, "I thirst." Holy Scripture remains the basis of our faith, established by every word and act of our Redeemer. The last word but one is, "It is finished." There is the complete justification of the believer, since the work by which he is accepted is fully accomplished. The last of his last words is also taken from the Scriptures, and shows where his mind was feeding. He cried, ere he bowed the head which he had held erect amid all his conflict, as one who never yielded, "Father, into thy hands I commend my spirit." In that cry there is reconciliation to God. He who stood in our stead has finished all his work, and now his spirit comes back to the Father, and he brings us with him. Every word, therefore, you see teaches us some grand fundamental doctrine of our blessed faith. "He that hath ears to hear, let him hear."

A second mode of treating these seven cries is to view them as setting forth the person and offices of our Lord who uttered them. "Father, forgive them; for they know not what they do"—here we see the Mediator interceding: Jesus standing before the Father pleading for the guilty. "Verily I say unto thee, to-day shalt thou be with me in paradise"—this is the Lord Jesus in kingly power, opening with the key of David a door which none can shut, admitting into the gates of heaven the poor soul who had confessed him on the tree. Hail, everlasting King in heaven, thou dost admit to thy paradise whomsoever thou wilt! Nor dost thou set a time for waiting, but instantly thou dost set wide the gate of pearl; thou hast all power in heaven as well as upon earth. Then came, "Woman, behold thy son!" wherein we see the Son of man in the gentleness of a son caring for his bereaved mother. In the former cry, as he opened Paradise, you saw the Son of God; now you see him who was verily and truly born of a woman, made under the law; and under the law you see him still, for he honours his mother and cares for her in the last article of death. Then comes the "My God, my God, why hast thou forsaken me?" Here we behold his human soul in anguish, his inmost heart overwhelmed by the withdrawing of Jehovah's face, and made to cry out as if in perplexity and amazement. "I thirst," is his human body tormented by grievous pain. Here you see how the mortal flesh had to share in the agony of the inward spirit. "It is finished" is the last word but one, and there you see the perfected Saviour, the Captain of our salvation, who has completed the undertaking upon which he had entered, finished transgression, made an end of sin, and brought in everlasting righteousness. The last expiring word in which he commended his spirit to his Father, is the note of acceptance for himself and for us all. As he commends his spirit into the Father's hand, so does he bring all believers nigh to God, and henceforth we are in the hand of the Father, who is greater than all, and none shall pluck us thence. Is not this a fertile field of thought? May the Holy Spirit often lead us to glean therein.

There are many other ways in which these words might be read, and they would be found to be all full of instruction. Like the steps of a ladder or the links of a golden chain, there is a mutual dependence and interlinking of each of the cries, so that one leads to another and that to a third. Separately or in connection our Master's words overflow with instruction to thoughtful minds: but of all save one I must say, "Of which we cannot now speak particularly."

Our text is the shortest of all the words of Calvary; it stands as two words in our language—"I thirst," but in the Greek it is only one. I cannot say that it is short and sweet, for, alas, it was bitterness itself to our Lord Jesus; and yet out of its bitterness I trust there will come great sweetness to us. Though bitter to him in the speaking it will be sweet to us in the hearing,—so sweet that all the bitterness of our trials shall be forgotten as we remember the vinegar and gall of which he drank.

We shall by the assistance of the Holy Spirit try to regard these words of our Saviour in a five-fold light. First, we shall look upon them as THE ENSIGN OF HIS TRUE HUMANITY. Jesus said, "I thirst," and this is the complaint of a man. Our Lord is the Maker of the ocean and the waters that are above the firmament: it is his hand that stays or opens the bottles of heaven, and sendeth rain upon the evil and upon the good. "The sea is his, and he made it," and all fountains and springs are of his digging. He poureth out the streams that run among the hills, the torrents which rush adown the mountains, and the flowing rivers which enrich the plains. One would have said, If he were thirsty he would not tell us, for all the clouds and rains would be glad to refresh his brow, and the brooks and streams would joyously flow at his feet. And yet, though he was Lord of all he had so fully taken upon himself the form of a servant and was so perfectly made in the likeness of sinful flesh, that he cried with fainting voice, "I thirst." How truly man he is; he is, indeed, "bone of our bone and flesh of our flesh," for he bears our infirmities. I invite you to meditate upon the true humanity of our

Lord very reverently, and very lovingly. Jesus was proved to be really man, because he suffered the pains which belong to manhood. Angels cannot suffer thirst. A phantom, as some have called him, could not suffer in this fashion: but Jesus really suffered, not only the more refined pains of delicate and sensitive minds, but the rougher and commoner pangs of flesh and blood. Thirst is a common-place misery, such as may happen to peasants or beggars; it is a real pain, and not a thing of a fancy or a nightmare of dreamland. Thirst is no royal grief, but an evil of universal manhood; Jesus is brother to the poorest and most humble of our race. Our Lord, however, endured thirst to an extreme degree, for it was the thirst of death which was upon him, and more, it was the thirst of one whose death was not a common one, for "he tasted death for every man." That thirst was caused, perhaps, in part by the loss of blood, and by the fever created by the irritation caused by his four grievous wounds. The nails were fastened in the most sensitive parts of the body, and the wounds were widened as the weight of his body dragged the nails through his blessed flesh, and tore his tender nerves. The extreme tension produced a burning feverishness. It was pain that dried his mouth and made it like an oven, till he declared, in the language of the twenty-second psalm, "My tongue cleaveth to my jaws." It was a thirst such as none of us have ever known, for not yet has the death dew condensed upon our brows. We shall perhaps know it in our measure in our dying hour, but not yet, nor ever so terribly as he did. Our Lord felt that grievous drought of dissolution by which all moisture seems dried up, and the flesh returns to the dust of death: this those know who have commenced to tread the valley of the shadow of death. Jesus, being a man, escaped none of the ills which are allotted to man in death. He is indeed "Immanuel, God with us" everywhere.

Believing this, let us tenderly feel how very near akin to us our Lord Jesus has become. You have been ill, and you have been parched with fever as he was, and then you too have gasped out "I thirst." Your path runs hard by that of your Master. He said, "I thirst," in order that some one might bring him drink, even as you have wished to have a cooling draught handed to you when you could not help yourself. Can you help feeling how very near Jesus is to us when his lips must be moistened with a sponge, and he must be so dependent upon others as to ask drink from their hand? Next time your fevered lips murmur "I am very thirsty," you may say to yourself, "Those are sacred words, for my Lord spake in that fashion." The words, "I thirst," are a common voice in death chambers. We can never forget the painful scenes of which we have been witness, when we have watched the dissolving of the human frame. Some of those whom we loved very dearly we have seen quite unable to help themselves; the death sweat has been upon them, and this has been one of the marks of their approaching dissolution, that they have been parched with thirst, and could only mutter between their half-closed lips, "Give me to drink." Ah, beloved, our

Lord was so truly man that all our griefs remind us of him: the next time we are thirsty we may gaze upon him; and whenever we see a friend faint and thirsting while dying we may behold our Lord dimly, but truly, mirrored in his members. How near akin the thirsty Saviour is to us; let us love him more and more.

How great the love which led him to such a condescension as this! Do not let us forget the infinite distance between the Lord of glory on his throne and the Crucified dried up with thirst. A river of the water of life, pure as crystal, proceedeth to-day out of the throne of God and of the Lamb, and yet once he condescended to say, "I thirst." He is Lord of fountains and all deeps, but not a cup of cold water was placed to his lips. Oh, if he had at any time said, "I thirst," before his angelic guards, they would surely have emulated the courage of the men of David when they cut their way to the well of Bethlehem that was within the gate, and drew water in jeopardy of their lives. Who among us would not willingly pour out his soul unto death if he might but give refreshment to the Lord? And yet he placed himself for our sakes into a position of shame and suffering where none would wait upon him, but when he cried, "I thirst," they gave him vinegar to drink. Glorious stoop of our exalted Head! O Lord Jesus, we love thee and we worship thee! We would fain lift thy name on high in grateful remembrance of the depths to which thou didst descend!

While thus we admire his condescension let our thoughts also turn with delight to his sure sympathy: for if Jesus said, "I thirst," then he knows all our frailties and woes. The next time we are in pain or are suffering depression of spirit we will remember that our Lord understands it all, for he has had practical, personal experience of it. Neither in torture of body nor in sadness of heart are we deserted by our Lord; his line is parallel with ours. The arrow which has lately pierced thee, my brother, was first stained with his blood. The cup of which thou art made to drink, though it be very bitter, bears the mark of his lips about its brim. He hath traversed the mournful way before thee, and every footprint thou leavest in the sodden soil is stamped side by side with his footmarks. Let the sympathy of Christ, then, be fully believed in and deeply appreciated, since he said, "I thirst."

Henceforth, also, let us cultivate the spirit of resignation, for we may well rejoice to carry a cross which his shoulders have borne before us. Beloved, if our Master said, "I thirst," do we expect every day to drink of streams from Lebanon? He was innocent, and yet he thirsted; shall we marvel if guilty ones are now and then chastened? If he was so poor that his garments were stripped from him, and he was hung up upon the tree, penniless and friendless, hungering and thirsting, will you henceforth groan and murmur because you bear the yoke of poverty and want? There is bread upon your table to-day, and there will be at least a cup of cold water to refresh you. You are not, therefore, so poor as he. Complain not, then. Shall the servant be above his Master, or the disciple above his Lord? Let patience have her perfect work. You do suffer. Perhaps, dear sister, you carry about with you a gnawing disease which eats at your heart, but Jesus took our sicknesses, and his cup was more bitter than yours. In your chamber let the gasp of your Lord as he said, "I thirst," go through your ears, and as you hear it let it touch your heart and cause you to gird up yourself and say, "Doth he say, 'I thirst'? Then I will thirst with him and not complain, I will suffer with him and not murmur." The Redeemer's cry of "I thirst" is a solemn lesson of patience to his afflicted.

Once again, as we think of this "I thirst," which proves our Lord's humanity, let us resolve to shun no denials, but rather court them that we may be conformed to his image. May we not be half ashamed of our pleasures when he says, "I thirst"? May we not despise our loaded table while he is so neglected? Shall it ever be a hardship to be denied the satisfying draught when he said, "I thirst." Shall carnal appetites be indulged and bodies pampered when Jesus cried "I thirst"? What if the bread be dry, what if the medicine be nauseous; yet for his thirst there was no relief but gall and vinegar, and dare we complain? For his sake we may rejoice in self-denials, and accept Christ and a crust as all we desire between here and heaven. A Christian living to indulge the base appetites of a brute beast, to eat and to drink almost to gluttony and drunkenness, is utterly unworthy of the name. The conquest of the appetites, the entire subjugation of the flesh, must be achieved, for before our great Exemplar said, "It is finished," wherein methinks he reached the greatest height of all, he stood as only upon the next lower step to that elevation, and said, "I thirst." The power to suffer for another, the capacity to be self-denying even to an extreme to accomplish some great work for God—this is a thing to be sought after, and must be gained before our work is done, and in this Jesus is before us our example and our strength.

Thus have I tried to spy out a measure of teaching, by using that one glass for the soul's eye, through which we look upon "I thirst" as the ensign of his true humanity.

II. Secondly, we shall regard these words, "I thirst," as THE TOKEN OF HIS SUFFERING SUBSTITUTION. The great Surety says, "I thirst," because he is placed in the sinner's stead, and he must therefore undergo the penalty of sin for the ungodly. "My God, my God, why hast thou forsaken me?" points to the anguish of his soul; "I thirst" expresses in part the torture of his body; and they were both needful, because it is written of the God of justice that he is "able to destroy both soul and body in hell," and the pangs that are due to law are of both kinds, touching both heart and flesh. See, brethren, where sin begins, and mark that there it ends. It began with the mouth of appetite, when it was sinfully gratified, and it ends when a kindred appetite is graciously denied. Our first parents plucked forbidden fruit, and by eating slew the race. Appetite was the door of sin, and therefore in that point our Lord was put to pain. With "I thirst" the evil is destroyed and receives its expiation. I saw the other day the emblem of a serpent with its tail in its mouth, and if I carry it a little beyond the artist's intention the symbol may set forth appetite swallowing up itself. A carnal appetite of the body, the satisfaction of the desire for food, first brought us down under the first Adam, and now the pang of thirst, the denial of what the body craved for, restores us to our place.

Nor is this all. We know from experience that the present effect of sin in every man who indulges in it is thirst of soul. The mind of man is like the daughters of the horseleech, which cry for ever "Give, give." Metaphorically understood, thirst is dissatisfaction, the craving of the mind for something which it has not, but which it pines for. Our Lord says, "If any man thirst, let him come unto me and drink," that thirst being the result of sin in every ungodly man at this moment. Now Christ standing in the stead of the ungodly suffers thirst as a type of his enduring the result of sin. More solemn still is the reflection that according to our Lord's own teaching, thirst will also be the eternal result of sin, for he says concerning the rich glutton, "In hell he lift up his eyes, being in torment," and his prayer, which was denied him, was, "Father Abraham, send Lazarus, that he may dip the tip of his finger in water and cool my tongue, for I am tormented in this flame." Now recollect, if Jesus had not thirsted, every one of us would have thirsted for ever afar off from God, with an impassable gulf between us and heaven. Our sinful tongues, blistered by the fever of passion, must have burned for ever had not his tongue been tormented with thirst in our stead. I suppose that the "I thirst" was uttered softly, so that perhaps only one and another who stood near the cross heard it at all; in contrast with the louder cry of "Lama sabachthani" and the triumphant shout of "It is finished": but that soft, expiring sigh, "I thirst," has ended for us the thirst which else, insatiably fierce, had preyed upon us throughout eternity. Oh, wondrous substitution of the just for the unjust, of God for man, of the perfect Christ for us guilty, hell-deserving rebels. Let us magnify and bless our Redeemer's name.

It seems to me very wonderful that this "I thirst" should be, as it were, the clearance of it all. He had no sooner said "I thirst," and sipped the vinegar, than he shouted, "It is finished"; and all was over: the battle was fought and the victory won for ever, and our great Deliverer's thirst was the sign of his having smitten the last foe. The flood of his grief had passed the high-water mark, and began to be assuaged. The "I thirst" was the bearing of the last pang; what if I say it was the expression of the fact that his pangs had at last begun to cease, and their fury had spent itself, and left him able to note his lesser pains? The excitement of a great struggle makes men forget thirst and faintness; it is only when all is over that they come back to themselves and note the spending of their strength. The great agony of being forsaken by God was over, and he felt faint when the strain was withdrawn. I like to think of our Lord's saying, "It is finished," directly after he had exclaimed, "I thirst"; for these two voices come so naturally together. Our glorious Samson had been fighting our foes; heaps upon heaps he had slain his thousands, and now like Samson he was sore athirst. He sipped of the vinegar, and he was refreshed, and no sooner has he thrown off the thirst than he shouted like a conqueror, "It is finished," and quitted the field, covered with renown. Let us exult as we see our Substitute going through with his work even to the bitter end, and then with a "Consummatum est" returning to his Father, God. O souls, burdened with sin, rest ye here, and resting live.

III. We will now take the text in a third way, and may the Spirit of God instruct us once again. The utterance of "I thirst" brought out A TYPE OF MAN'S TREATMENT OF HIS LORD. It was a confirmation of the Scripture testimony with regard to man's natural enmity to God. According to modern thought man is a very fine and noble creature, struggling to become better. He is greatly to be commended and admired, for his sin is said to be a seeking after God, and his superstition is a struggling after light. Great and worshipful being that he is, truth is to be altered for him, the gospel is to be modulated to suit the tone of his various generations, and all the arrangements of the universe are to be rendered subservient to his interests. Justice must fly the field lest it be severe to so deserving a being; as for punishment, it must not be whispered to his ears polite. In fact, the tendency is to exalt man above God and give him the highest place. But such is not the truthful estimate of man according to the Scriptures: there man is a fallen creature, with a carnal mind which cannot be reconciled to God; a worse than brutish creature, rendering evil for good, and treating his God with vile ingratitude. Alas, man is the slave and the dupe of Satan, and a black-hearted traitor to his God. Did not the prophecies say that man would give to his incarnate God gall to eat and vinegar to drink? It is done. He came to save, and man denied him hospitality: at the first there was no room for him at the inn, and at the last there was not one cool cup of water for him to drink; but when he thirsted they gave him vinegar to drink. This is man's treatment of his Saviour. Universal manhood, left to itself, rejects, crucifies, and mocks the Christ of God. This was the act too of man at his best, when he is moved to pity; for it seems clear that he who lifted up the wet sponge to the Redeemer's lips, did it in compassion. I think that Roman soldier meant well, at least well for a rough warrior with his little light and knowledge. He ran and filled a sponge with vinegar: it was the best way he knew of putting a few drops of moisture to the lips of one who was suffering so much; but though he felt a degree of pity, it was such as one might show to a dog; he felt no reverence, but mocked as he relieved. We read, "The soldiers also mocked him, offering him vinegar." When our Lord cried, "Eloi, Eloi," and afterwards said, "I thirst," the persons around the cross said, "Let be, let us see whether Elias will come to save him," mocking him; and, according to Mark, he who gave the vinegar uttered much the same words. He pitied the sufferer, but he thought so little of him that he joined in the voice of scorn. Even when man compassionates the sufferings of Christ, and man would have ceased to be human if he did not, still he scorns him; the very cup which man gives to Jesus is at once scorn and pity, for "the tender mercies of the wicked are cruel." See how man at his best mingles admiration of the Saviour's person with scorn of his claims; writing books to hold him up as an example and at the same moment rejecting his deity; admitting that he was a wonderful man, but denying his most sacred mission; extolling his ethical teaching and then trampling on his blood: thus giving him drink, but that drink vinegar. O my hearers, beware of praising Jesus and denying his atoning sacrifice. Beware of rendering him homage and dishonouring his name at the same time.

Alas, my brethren, I cannot say much on the score of man's cruelty to our Lord without touching myself and you. Have we not often given him vinegar to drink? Did we not do so years ago before we knew him? We used to melt when we heard about his sufferings, but we did not turn from our sins. We gave him our tears and then grieved him with our sins. We thought sometimes that we loved him as we heard the story of his death, but we did not change our lives for his sake, nor put our trust in him, and so we gave him vinegar to drink. Nor does the grief end here, for have not the best works we have ever done, and the best feelings we have ever felt, and the best prayers we have ever offered, been tart and sour with sin? Can they be compared to generous wine? are they not more like sharp vinegar? I wonder he has ever received them, as one marvels why he received this vinegar; and yet he has received them, and smiled upon us for presenting them. He knew once how to turn water into wine, and in matchless love he has often turned our sour drink-offerings into something sweet to himself, though in themselves, methinks, they have been the juice of sour grapes, sharp enough to set his teeth on edge. We may therefore come before him, with all the rest of our race, when God subdues them to repentance by his love, and look on him whom we have pierced, and mourn for him as one that is in bitterness for his firstborn. We may well remember our faults this day,

> "We, whose proneness to forget
> Thy dear love, on Olivet
> Bathed thy brow with bloody sweat;
> "We, whose sins, with awful power,
> Like a cloud did o'er thee lower,
> In that God-excluding hour;
> "We, who still, in thought and deed,
> Often hold the bitter reed
> To thee, in thy time of need."

I have touched that point very lightly because I want a little more time to dwell upon a fourth view of this scene. May the Holy Ghost help us to hear a fourth tuning of the dolorous music, "I thirst."

IV. I think, beloved friends, that the cry of "I thirst" was THE MYSTICAL EXPRESSION OF THE DESIRE OF HIS HEART—"I thirst." I cannot think that natural thirst was all he felt. He thirsted for water doubtless, but his soul was thirsty in a higher sense; indeed, he seems only to have spoken that the Scriptures might be fulfilled as to the offering him vinegar. Always was he in harmony with himself, and his body was always expressive of his soul's cravings as well as of its own longings. "I thirst" meant that his heart was thirsting to save men. This thirst had been on him from the earliest of his earthly days. "Wist ye not," said he, while yet a boy, "that I must be about my Father's business?" Did he not tell his disciples, "I have a baptism to be baptized with, and how am I straitened till it be accomplished?" He thirsted to pluck us from between the jaws of hell, to pay our redemption price, and set us free from the eternal condemnation which hung over us; and when on the cross the work was almost done his thirst was not assuaged, and could not be till he could say, "It is finished." It is almost done, thou Christ of God; thou hast almost saved thy people; there remaineth but one thing more, that thou shouldst actually die, and hence thy strong desire to come to the end and complete thy labour. Thou wast still straitened till the last pang was felt and the last word spoken to complete the full redemption, and hence thy cry, "I thirst."

Beloved, there is now upon our Master, and there always has been, a thirst after the love of his people. Do you not remember how that thirst of his was strong in the old days of the prophet? Call to mind his complaint in the fifth chapter of Isaiah, "Now will I sing to my wellbeloved a song of my beloved touching his vineyard. My wellbeloved hath a vineyard in a very fruitful hill: and he fenced it, and gathered out the stones thereof, and planted it with the choicest vine, and built a tower in the midst of it, and also made a winepress therein." What was he looking for from his vineyard and its winepress? What but for the juice of the vine that he might be refreshed? "And he looked that it should bring forth grapes, and it brought forth wild grapes,"—vinegar, and not wine; sourness, and not sweetness. So he was thirsting then. According to the sacred canticle of love, in the fifth chapter of the Song of Songs, we learn that when he drank in those olden times it was in the garden of his church that he was refreshed. What doth he say? "I am come into my garden, my sister, my spouse: I have gathered my myrrh with my spice; I have eaten my honeycomb with my honey; I have drunk my wine with my milk; eat, O friends; drink, yea, drink abundantly, O beloved." In the same song he speaks of his church, and says, "The roof of thy mouth is as the best wine for my beloved, that goeth down sweetly, causing the lips of those that are asleep to speak." And yet again in the eighth chapter the bride saith, "I would cause thee to drink of spiced wine of the juice of my pomegranate." Yes, he loves to be with his people; they are the garden where he walks for refreshment, and their love, their graces, are the milk and wine of which he delights to drink. Christ was always thirsty to save men, and to be loved of men; and we see a type of his life-long desire when, being weary, he sat thus on the well and said to the woman of Samaria, "Give me to drink." There was a deeper meaning in his words than she dreamed of, as a verse further down fully proves, when he said to his disciples, "I have meat to eat that ye know not of." He derived spiritual refreshment from the winning of that woman's heart to himself.

And now, brethren, our blessed Lord has at this time a thirst for communion with each one of you who are his people, not because you can do him good, but because he can do you good. He thirsts to bless you and to receive your grateful love in return; he thirsts to see you looking with believing eye to his fulness, and holding out your emptiness that he may supply it. He saith, "Behold, I stand at the door and knock." What knocks he for? It is that he may eat and drink with you, for he promises that if we open to him he will enter in and sup with us and we with him. He is thirsty still, you see, for our poor love, and surely we cannot deny it to him. Come let us pour out full flagons, until his joy is fulfilled in us. And what makes him love us so? Ah, that I cannot tell, except his own great love. He must love; it is his nature. He must love his chosen whom he has once begun to love, for he is the same yesterday, to-day, and for ever. His great love makes him thirst to have us much nearer than we are; he will never be satisfied till all his redeemed are beyond gunshot of the enemy. I will give you one of his thirsty prayers—"Father, I will that they also whom thou hast given me be with me where I am, that they may behold my glory." He wants you brother, he wants you, dear sister, he longs to have you wholly to himself. Come to him in prayer, come to him in fellowship, come to him by perfect consecration, come to him by surrendering your whole being to the sweet mysterious influences of his Spirit. Sit at his feet with Mary, lean on his breast with John; yea, come with the spouse in the song and say, "Let him kiss me with the kisses of his mouth, for his love is better than wine." He calls for that: will you not give it to him? Are you so frozen at heart that not a cup of cold water can be melted for Jesus? Are you lukewarm? O brother, if he says, "I thirst" and you bring him a lukewarm heart, that is worse than vinegar, for he has said, "I will spue thee out of my mouth." He can receive vinegar, but not lukewarm love. Come, bring him your warm heart, and let him drink from that purified chalice as much as he wills. Let all your love be his. I know he loves to receive from you, because he delights even in a cup of cold water that you give to one of his disciples; how much more will he delight in the giving of your whole self to him? Therefore while he thirsts give him to drink this day.

V. Lastly, the cry of "I thirst" is to us THE PATTERN OF OUR DEATH WITH HIM. Know ye not, beloved,—for I speak to those who know the Lord,—that ye are crucified together with Christ? Well, then, what means this cry, "I thirst," but this, that we should thirst too? We do not thirst after the old manner wherein we were bitterly afflicted, for he hath said, "He that drinketh of this water shall never thirst:" but now we covet a new thirst, a refined and heavenly appetite, a craving for our Lord. O thou blessed Master, if we are indeed nailed up to the tree with thee, give us to thirst after thee with a thirst which only the cup of "the new covenant in thy blood" can ever satisfy. Certain philosophers have said that they love the pursuit of truth even better than the knowledge of truth. I differ from them greatly, but I will say this, that next to the actual enjoyment of my Lord's presence I love to hunger and to thirst after him. Rutherford used words somewhat to this effect, "I thirst for my Lord and this is joy; a joy which no man taketh from me. Even if I may not come at him, yet shall I be full of consolation, for it is heaven to thirst after him, and surely he will never deny a poor soul liberty to admire him, and adore him, and thirst after him." As for myself, I would grow more and more insatiable after my divine Lord, and when I have much of him I would still cry for more; and then for more, and still for more. My heart shall not be content till he is all in all to me, and I am altogether lost in him. O to be enlarged in soul so as to take deeper draughts of his sweet love, for our heart cannot have enough. One would wish to be as the spouse, who, when she had already been feasting in the banqueting-house, and had found his fruit sweet to her taste, so that she was overjoyed, yet cried out, "Stay me with flagons, comfort me with apples, for I am sick of love." She craved full flagons of love though she was already overpowered by it. This is a kind of sweet whereof if a man hath much he must have more, and when he hath more he is under a still greater necessity to receive more, and so on, his appetite for ever growing by that which it feeds upon, till he is filled with all the fulness of God. "I thirst,"—ay, this is my soul's word with her Lord. Borrowed from his lips it well suiteth my mouth.

> "I thirst, but not as once I did,
> The vain delights of earth to share;
> Thy wounds, Emmanuel, all forbid
> That I should seek my pleasures there.
> "Dear fountain of delight unknown!
> No longer sink below the brim;
> But overflow, and pour me down
> A living and life-giving stream."

Jesus thirsted, then let us thirst in this dry and thirsty land where no water is. Even as the hart panteth after the water brooks, our souls would thirst after thee, O God.

Beloved, let us thirst for the souls of our fellow-men. I have already told you that such was our Lord's mystical desire; let it be ours also. Brother, thirst to have your children saved. Brother, thirst I pray you to have your workpeople saved. Sister, thirst for the salvation of your class, thirst for the redemption of your family thirst for the conversion of your husband. We ought all to have a longing for conversions. Is it so with each one of you? If not, bestir yourselves at once. Fix your hearts upon some unsaved one, and thirst until he is saved. It is the way whereby many shall be brought to Christ, when this blessed soul-thirst of true Christian charity shall be upon those who are themselves saved. Remember how Paul said, "I say the truth in Christ, I lie not, my conscience also bearing me witness in the Holy Ghost, that I have great heaviness and continual sorrow in my heart. For I could wish that myself were accursed from Christ for my brethren, my kinsmen according to the flesh." He would have sacrificed himself to save his countrymen, so heartily did he desire their eternal welfare. Let this mind be in you also.

As for yourselves, thirst after perfection. Hunger and thirst after righteousness, for you shall be filled. Hate sin, and heartily loathe it; but thirst to be holy as God is holy, thirst to be like Christ, thirst to bring glory to his sacred name by complete conformity to his will.

May the Holy Ghost work in you the complete pattern of Christ crucified, and to him shall be praise for ever and ever. Amen.

Delivered on the Lord's-Day Morning, April 14, 1878. Originally titled, "The Shortest of the Seven Cries."

5
IT IS FINISHED!

"When Jesus therefore had received the vinegar, he said, It is finished: and he bowed his head, and gave up the ghost."

—*John 19:30*

—

MY brethren, I would have you attentively observe the singular clearness, power, and quickness of the Saviour's mind in the last agonies of death. When pains and groans attend the last hour, they frequently have the effect of discomposing the mind, so that it is not possible for the dying man to collect his thoughts, or having collected them, to utter them so that they can be understood by others. In no case could we expect a remarkable exercise of memory, or a profound judgment upon deep subjects from an expiring man. But the Redeemer's last acts were full of wisdom and prudence, although his sufferings were beyond all measure excruciating. Remark how clearly he perceived the significance of every type! How plainly he could read with dying eye those divine symbols which the eyes of angels could only desire to look into! He saw the secrets which have bewildered sages and astonished seers, all fulfilled in his own body. Nor must we fail to observe the power and comprehensiveness by which he grasped the chain which binds the shadowy past with the sun-lit present. We must not forget the brilliance of that intelligence which threaded all the ceremonies and sacrifices on one string of thought, beheld all the prophecies as one great revelation, and all the promises as the heralds of one person, and then said of the whole, " 'It is finished,' finished in me." What quickness of mind was that which enabled him to traverse all the centuries of prophecy; to penetrate the eternity of the covenant, and then to anticipate the eternal glories! And all this when he is mocked by multitudes of enemies, and when his hands and feet are nailed to the cross! What force of mind must the Saviour have possessed, to soar above those Alps of Agony, which touched the very clouds. In what a singular mental condition must he have been during the period of his crucifixion, to be able to review the whole roll of inspiration! Now, this remark may not seem to be of any great value, but I think its value lies in certain inferences that may be drawn from it. We have sometimes heard it said, "How could Christ, in so short a time, bear suffering which should be equivalent to the torments—the eternal torments of hell?" Our reply is, we are not capable of judging what the Son of God might do even in a moment, much less what he might do and what he might suffer in his life and in his death. It has been frequently affirmed by persons who have been rescued from drowning, that the mind of a drowning man is singularly active. One who, after being some time in the water, was at last painfully restored, said that the whole of his history seemed to come before his mind while he was sinking, and that if any one had asked him how long he had been in the water, he should have said twenty years, whereas he had only been there for a moment or two. The wild romance of Mahomet's journey upon Alborak is not an unfitting illustration. He affirmed that when the angel came in vision to take him on his celebrated journey to Jerusalem, he went through all the seven heavens, and saw all the wonders thereof, and yet he was gone so short a time, that though the angel's wing had touched a basin of water when they started, they returned soon enough to prevent the water from being spilt. The long dream of the epileptic impostor may really have occupied but a second of time. The intellect of mortal man is such that, if God wills it, when it is in certain states, it can think out centuries of thought at once; it can go through in one instant what we should have supposed would have taken years upon years of time for it to know or feel. We think, therefore, that from the Saviour's singular clearness and quickness of intellect upon the cross, it is very possible that he did in the space of two or three hours endure not only the agony which might have been contained in centuries, but even an equivalent for that which might be comprehended in everlasting punishment. At any rate, it is not for us to say that it could not be so. When the Deity is arrayed in manhood, then manhood becomes omnipotent to suffer; and just as the feet of Christ were once almighty to tread the seas, so now was his whole body become almighty to dive into the great waters, to endure an immersion in "unknown agonies." Do not, I pray you, let us attempt to measure Christ's sufferings by the finite line of your own ignorant reason, but let us know and believe that what he endured there was accepted by God as an equivalent for all our pains, and therefore it could not have been a trifle, but must have been all that Hart conceived it to be, when he says He bore—

> "All that incarnate God could bear,
> With strength enough, but none to spare."

My discourse will, I have no doubt, more fully illustrate the remark with which I have commenced; let us proceed to it at once. First, let us hear the text and understand it; then let us hear it and wonder at it; and then, thirdly, let us hear it and proclaim it.

I. LET US HEAR THE TEXT AND UNDERSTAND IT.

The Son of God has been made man. He has lived a life of perfect virtue and of total self-denial. He has been all that life long despised and rejected of men, a man of sorrows and acquainted with grief. His enemies have been legion; his friends have been few, and those few faithless. He is at last delivered over into the hands of them that hate him. He is arrested while in the act of prayer; he is arraigned before both the spiritual and temporal courts. He is robed in mockery, and then unrobed in shame. He is set upon his throne in scorn, and then tied to the pillar in cruelty. He is declared innocent, and yet he is delivered up by the judge who ought to have preserved him from his persecutors. He is dragged through the streets of that Jerusalem which had killed the prophets, and would now crimson itself with the blood of the prophets' Master. He is brought to the cross; he is nailed fast to the cruel wood. The sun burns him. His cruel wounds increase the fever. God forsakes him. "My God, my God, why hast thou forsaken me?" contains the concentrated anguish of the world. While he hangs there in mortal conflict with sin and Satan, his heart is broken, his limbs are dislocated. Heaven fails him, for the sun is veiled in darkness. Earth forsakes him, for "his disciples forsook him and fled." He looks everywhere, and there is none to help; he casts his eye around, and there is no man that can share his toil. He treads the winepress alone; and of the people there is none with him. On, on, he goes, steadily determined to drink the last dreg of that cup which must not pass from him if his Father's will be done. At last he cries—"It is finished," and he gives up the ghost. Hear it, Christians, hear this shout of triumph as it rings to-day with all the freshness and force which it had eighteen hundred years ago! Hear it from the Sacred

Word, and from the Saviour's lips, and may the Spirit of God open your ears that you may hear as the learned, and understand what you hear!

1. What meant the Saviour, then, by this—"It is finished?" He meant, first of all, that all the types, promises, and prophecies were now fully accomplished in him. Those who are acquainted with the original will find that the words—"It is finished," occur twice within three verses. In the 28th verse, we have the word in the Greek; it is translated in our version "accomplished," but there it stands—"After this, Jesus knowing that all things were now finished, that the Scripture might be fulfilled, saith, I thirst." And then he afterwards said, "It is finished." This leads us to see his meaning very clearly, that all the Scripture was now fulfilled, that when he said, "It is finished," the whole book, from the first to the last, in both the law and the prophets, was finished in him. There is not a single jewel of promise, from that first emerald which fell on the threshold of Eden, to that last sapphire-stone of Malachi, which was not set in the breast-plate of the true High Priest. Nay, there is not a type, from the red heifer downward to the turtle-dove, from the hyssop upwards to Solomon's temple itself, which was not fulfilled in him; and not a prophecy, whether spoken on Chebar's bank, or on the shores of Jordan; not a dream of wise men, whether they had received it in Babylon, or in Samaria, or in Judea, which was not now fully wrought out in Christ Jesus. And, brethren, what a wonderful thing it is, that a mass of promises, and

prophecies, and types, apparently so heterogeneous, should all be accomplished in one person! Take away Christ for one moment, and I will give the Old Testament to any wise man living, and say to him, "Take this; this is a problem; go home and construct in your imagination an ideal character who shall exactly fit all that which is herein foreshadowed; remember, he must be a prophet like unto Moses, and yet a champion like to Joshua; he must be an Aaron and a Melchisedek; he must be both David and Solomon, Noah and Jonah, Judah and Joseph. Nay, he must not only be the lamb that was slain, and the scape-goat that was not slain, the turtle-dove that was dipped in blood, and the priest who slew the bird, but he must be the altar, the tabernacle, the mercy-seat, and the shewbread." Nay, to puzzle this wise man further, we remind him of prophecies so apparently contradictory, that one would think they never could meet in one man. Such as these, "All kings shall fall down before him, and all nations shall serve him;" and yet, "He is despised and rejected of men." He must begin by showing a man born of a virgin mother—"A virgin shall conceive and bear a son." He must be a man without spot or blemish, but yet one upon whom the Lord doth cause to meet the iniquities of us all. He must be a glorious one, a Son of David, but yet a root out of a dry ground. Now, I say it boldly, if all the greatest intellects of all the ages could set themselves to work out this problem, to invent another key to the types and prophecies, they could not do it. I see you, ye wise men, ye are poring over these hieroglyphs; one suggests one key, and it opens two or three of the figures, but you cannot proceed, for the next one puts you at a nonplus. Another learned man suggests another clue, but that fails most where it is most needed, and another, and another, and thus these wondrous hieroglyphs traced of old by Moses in the wilderness, must be left unexplained, till one comes forward and proclaims, "The cross of Christ and the Son of God incarnate," then the whole is clear, so that he that runs may read, and a child may understand. Blessed Saviour! In thee we see everything fulfilled, which God spoke of old by the prophets; in thee we discover everything carried out in substance, which God had set forth us in the dim mist of sacrificial smoke. Glory be unto thy name! "It is finished"—everything is summed up in thee.

2. But the words have richer meaning. Not only were all types, and prophecies, and promises thus finished in Christ, but all the typical sacrifices of the old Jewish law, were now abolished as well as explained. They were finished—finished in him. Will you imagine for a minute the saints in heaven looking down upon what was done on earth—Abel and his friends who had long ago before the flood been sitting in the glories above. They watch while God lights star after star in heaven. Promise after promise flashes light upon the thick darkness of earth. They see Abraham come, and they look down and wonder while they see God revealing Christ to Abraham in the person of Isaac. They gaze just as the angels do, desiring to look into the mystery. From the times of

Noah, Abraham, Isaac, and Jacob, they see altars smoking, recognitions of the fact that man is guilty, and the spirits before the throne say, "Lord, when will sacrifices finish?—when will blood no more be shed?" The offering of bloody sacrifices soon increases. It is now carried on by men ordained for the purpose. Aaron and the high priests, and the Levites, every morning and every evening offer a lamb, while great sacrifices are offered on special occasions. Bullocks groan, rams bleed, the necks of doves are wrung, and all the while the saints are crying, "O Lord, how long?—when shall the sacrifice cease?" Year after year the high priest goes within the veil and sprinkles the mercy-seat with blood; the next year sees him do the like, and the next, and again, and again, and again. David offers hecatombs, Solomon slaughters tens of thousands, Hezekiah offers rivers of oil, Josiah gives thousands of the fat of fed beasts, and the spirits of the just say, "Will it never be complete?—will the sacrifice never be finished?—must there always be a remembrance of sin?—will not the last High priest soon come?—will not the order and line of Aaron soon lay aside its labour, because the whole is finished?" Not yet, not yet, ye spirits of the just, for after the captivity the slaughter of victims still remains. But lo, he comes! Gaze more intently than before—He comes who is to close the line of priests! Lo! there he stands, clothed—not now with linen ephod, not with ringing bells, nor with sparkling jewels on his breastplate—but arrayed in human flesh he stands, his cross his altar, his body and his soul the victim, himself the priest, and lo! before his God he offers up his own soul within the veil of thick darkness which hath covered him from the sight of men. Presenting his own blood, he enters within the veil, sprinkles it there, and coming forth from the midst of the darkness, he looks down on the astonished earth, and upward to expectant heaven, and cries, "It is finished! it is finished!"—that for which ye looked so long, is fully achieved and perfected for ever.

3. The Saviour meant, we doubt not, that in this moment his perfect obedience was finished. It was necessary, in order that man might be saved, that the law of God should be kept, for no man can see God's face except he be perfect in righteousness. Christ undertook to keep God's law for his people, to obey its every mandate, and preserve its every statute intact. Throughout the first years of his life he privately obeyed, honouring his father and his mother; during the next three years he publicly obeyed God, spending and being spent in his service, till if you would know what a man would be whose life was wholly conformed to the law of God, you may see him in Christ.

> "My dear Redeemer and my Lord,
> I read my duty in thy word,
> But in thy life the law appears
> Drawn out in living characters."

It needed nothing to complete the perfect virtue of life but the entire obedience of death. He who would serve God must be willing not only to give all his soul and his strength while he lives, but he must stand prepared to resign life when it shall be for God's glory. Our perfect substitute put the last stroke upon his work by dying, and therefore he claims to be absolved from further debt, for "it is finished." Yes, glorious Lamb of God, it is finished I Thou hast been tempted in all points like as we are, yet hast thou sinned in none! It was finished, for the last arrow out of Satan's quiver had been shot at thee; the last blasphemous insinuation, the last wicked temptation had spent its fury on thee; the Prince of this world had surveyed thee from head to foot, within and without, but he had found nothing in thee. Now thy trial is over, thou hast finished the work which thy Father gave thee to do, and so finished it that hell itself cannot accuse thee of a flaw. And now, looking upon thine entire obedience, thou sayest, "It is finished," and we thy people believe most joyously that it is even so. Brothers and sisters, this is more than you or I could have said if Adam had never fallen. If we had been in the garden of Eden to-day, we could never have boasted a finished righteousness, since a creature can never finish its obedience. As long as a creature lives it is bound to obey, and as long as a free agent exists on earth it would be in danger of violating the vow of its obedience. If Adam had been in Paradise from the first day until now, he might fall to-morrow. Left to himself there would be no reason why that king of nature should not yet be uncrowned. But Christ the Creator, who finished creation, has perfected redemption. God can ask no more. The law has received all it claims; the largest extent of justice cannot demand another hour's obedience. It is done; it is complete; the last throw of the shuttle is over, and the robe is woven from the top throughout. Let us rejoice, then, in this that the Master meant by his dying cry that his perfect righteousness wherewith he covers us was finished.

4. But next, the Saviour meant that the satisfaction which he rendered to the justice of God was finished. The debt was now, to the last farthing, all discharged. The atonement and propitiation were made once for all, and for ever, by the one offering made in Jesu's body on the tree. There was the cup; hell was in it; the Saviour drank it—not a sip and then a pause; not a draught and then a ceasing; but he drained it till there is not a dreg left for any of his people. The great ten-thonged whip of the law was worn out upon his back; there is no lash left with which to smite one for whom Jesus died. The great cannonade of God's justice has exhausted all its ammunition; there is nothing left to be hurled against a child of God. Sheathed is thy sword, O Justice! Silenced is thy thunder, O Law! There remaineth nothing now of all the griefs, and pains, and agonies which chosen sinners ought to have suffered for their sins, for Christ has endured all for his own beloved, and "it is finished." Brethren, it is more than the damned in hell can ever say. If you and I had been constrained to make satisfaction to God's justice by being sent to hell we never could have said, "It is finished." Christ has paid the debt which all the torments of eternity could not have paid. Lost souls, ye suffer to-day as ye

have suffered for ages past, but God's justice is not satisfied; his law is not fully magnified. And when time shall fail, and eternity shall have been flying on, still for ever, for ever, the uttermost farthing never having been paid, the chastisement for sin must fall upon unpardoned sinners. But Christ has done what all the flames of the pit could not do in all eternity; he has magnified the law and made it honourable, and now from the cross he cries—"It is finished."

5. Once again: when he said, "It is finished," Jesus had totally destroyed the power of Satan, of sin, and of death. The champion had entered the lists to do battle for our soul's redemption, against all our foes. He met Sin. Horrible, terrible, all-but omnipotent Sin nailed him to the cross; but in that deed, Christ nailed Sin also to the tree. There they both did hang together—Sin, and Sin's destroyer. Sin destroyed Christ, and by that destruction Christ destroyed Sin. Next came the second enemy, Satan. He assaulted Christ with ail his hosts. Calling up his myrmidons from every corner and quarter of the universe, he said, "Awake, arise, or be for ever fallen! Here is our great enemy who has sworn to bruise my head; now let us bruise his heel!" They shot their hellish darts into his heart; they poured their boiling cauldrons on his brain; they emptied their venom into his veins; they spat their insinuations into his face; they hissed their devilish fears into his ear. He stood alone, the lion of the tribe of Judah, hounded by all the dogs of hell. Our champion quailed not, but used his holy weapons, striking right and left with all the power of

God-supported manhood. On came the hosts; volley after volley was discharged against him. No mimic thunders were these, but such as might shake the very gates of hell. The conqueror steadily advanced, overturning their ranks, dashing in pieces his enemies, breaking the bow and cutting the spear in sunder, and burning the chariots in the fire, while he cried, "In the name of God will I destroy ye!" At last, foot to foot, he met the champion of hell, and now our David fought with Goliath. Not long was the struggle; thick was the darkness which gathered round them both; but he who is the Son of God as well as the Son of Mary, knew how to smite the fiend, and he did smite him with divine fury, till, having despoiled him of his armour, having quenched his fiery darts, and broken his head, he cried, "It is finished," and sent the fiend, bleeding and howling, down to hell. We can imagine him pursued by the eternal Saviour, who exclaims:—

> "Traitor!
> My bolt shalt find and pierce thee through,
> Though under hell's profoundest wave
> Thou div'st, to seek a shelt'ring grave."

His thunderbolt o'ertook the fiend, and grasping him with both his hands, the Saviour drew around him the great chain. The angels brought the royal chariot from on high, to whose wheels the captive fiend was bound. Lash the coursers up the everlasting hills! Spirits made perfect come forth to meet him. Hymn the conqueror who drags death and hell behind him, and leads captivity captive! "Lift up your heads, O ye gates, and be ye lifted up, ye everlasting doors, that the King of glory may come in!" But stay; ere he enters, let him be rid of this his burden. Lo! he takes the fiend, and hurls him down through illimitable night, broken, bruised, with his power destroyed, bereft of his crown, to lie for ever howling in the pit of hell. Thus, when the Saviour cried, "It is finished," he had defeated Sin and Satan; nor less had he vanquished Death. Death had come against him, as Christmas Evans puts it, with his fiery dart, which he struck right through the Saviour, till the point fixed in the cross, and when he tried to pull it out again, he left the sting behind. What could he do more? He was disarmed. Then Christ set some of his prisoners free; for many of the saints arose and were seen of many: then he said to him, "Death, I take from thee thy keys; thou must live for a little while to be the warder of those beds in which my saints shall sleep, but give me thy keys." And lo! the Saviour stands to-day with the keys of death hanging at his girdle, and he waits until the hour shall come of which no man knoweth; when the trump of the archangel shall ring like the silver trumpets of Jubilee, and then he shall say, "Let my captives go free." Then shall the tombs be opened in virtue of Christ's death, and the very bodies of the saints shall live again in an eternity of glory.

> " 'It is finish'd!'
> Hear the dying Saviour cry."

II. Secondly, LET US HEAR AND WONDER.

Let us perceive what mighty things were effected and secured by these words, "It is finished." Thus he ratified the covenant. That covenant was signed and sealed before, and in all things it was ordered well, but when Christ said, "It is finished," then the covenant was made doubly sure; when the blood of Christ's heart bespattered the divine roll, then it could never be reversed, nor could one of its ordinances be broken, nor one of its stipulations fail. You know the covenant was on this wise. God covenants on his part that he would give Christ to see of the travail of his soul; that all who were given to him should have new hearts and right spirits; that they should be washed from sin, and should enter into life through him. Christ's side of the covenant was this—"Father, I will do thy will; I will pay the ransom to the last jot and tittle; I will give thee perfect obedience and complete satisfaction." Now if this second part of the covenant had never been fulfilled, the first part would have been invalid, but when Jesus said, "It is finished," then there was nothing left to be performed on his part, and now the covenant is all on one side. It is God's "I will," and "They shall." "A new heart will I give you, and a right spirit will I put within you." "I will sprinkle clean water upon you and ye shall be clean." "From all your iniquities will I cleanse you." "I will lead you by a way that ye know not." "I will surely bring them in." The covenant that day was ratified. When Christ said, "It is finished," his Father was honoured, and divine justice was fully displayed. The Father always did love his people. Do not think that Christ died to make God the Father loving. He always had loved them from before the foundation of the world, but—"It is finished," took away the barriers which were in the Father's way. He would, as a God of love, and now he could as a God of justice, bless poor sinners. From that day the Father is well pleased to receive sinners to his bosom. When Christ said—"It is finished," he himself was glorified. Then on his head descended the all-glorious crown. Then did the Father give to him honours, which he had not before. He had honour as God, but as man he was despised and rejected; now as God and man Christ was made to sit down for ever on his Father's throne, crowned with honour and majesty. Then, too, by "It is finished," the Spirit was procured for us.

> "'Tis by the merit of his death
>   Who hung upon the tree,
> The Spirit is sent down to breathe
>   On such dry bones as we."

Then the Spirit which Christ had aforetime promised, perceived a new and living way by which he could come to dwell in the hearts of men, and men might come up to dwell with him above. That day too, when Christ said—"It is finished," the words had effect on heaven. Then the walls of chrysolite stood fast; then the jasper-light of the pearly-gated city shone like the light of seven days. Before, the saints had been saved as it were on credit. They had entered heaven, God having faith in his Son Jesus. Had not Christ finished his work, surely they must have left their shining spheres, and suffered in their own persons for their own sins. I might represent heaven, if my imagination might be allowed a moment, as being ready to totter if Christ had not finished his work; its stones would have been unloosed; massive and stupendous though its bastions are, yet had they fallen as earthly cities reel under the throes of earthquake. But Christ said, "It is finished," and oath, and covenant, and blood set fast the dwelling-place of the redeemed, made their mansions safely and eternally their own, and bade their feet stand immoveably upon the rock. Nay, more, that word "It is finished!" took effect in the gloomy caverns and depths of HELL. Then Satan bit his iron bands in rage, howling, "I am defeated by the very man whom I thought to overcome; my hopes are blasted; never shall an elect one come into my prison-house, never a blood-bought one be found in my abode." Lost souls mourned that day, for they said— " 'It is finished!' and if Christ himself, the substitute, could not be permitted to go free till he had finished all his punishment, then we shall never be free." It was their double death-knell, for they said, "Alas for us! Justice, which would not suffer the Saviour to escape, will never suffer us to be at liberty. It is finished with him, and therefore it shall never be finished for us." That day, too, the earth had a gleam of sunlight cast over her which she had never known before. Then her hill-tops began to glisten with the rising of the sun, and though her valleys still are clothed with darkness, and men wander hither and thither, and grope in the noonday as in the night, yet that sun is rising, climbing still its heavenly steeps, never to set, and soon shall its rays penetrate through the thick mists and clouds, and every eye shall see him, and every heart be made glad with his light. The words "It is finished!" consolidated heaven, shook hell, comforted earth, delighted the Father, glorified the Son, brought down the Spirit, and confirmed the everlasting covenant to all the chosen seed.

III. And now I come to my last point, upon which very briefly. "It is finished!" LET US PUBLISH IT.

Children of God, ye who by faith received Christ as your all in all, tell it every day of your lives that "it is finished." Go and tell it to those who are torturing themselves, thinking through obedience and mortification to offer satisfaction. Yonder Hindoo is about to throw himself down upon the spikes. Stay, poor man! wherefore wouldst thou bleed, for "it is finished"? Yonder Fakir is holding his hand erect till the nails grow through the flesh, torturing himself with fastings and with self-denials. Cease, cease, poor wretch, from all these pains, for "it is finished!" In all parts of the earth there are those who think that the misery of the body and the soul may be an atonement for sin. Rush to them, stay them in their madness and say to them, "Wherefore do ye this? 'It is finished.'" All the pains that God asks, Christ has suffered; all the satisfaction by way of agony in the flesh that the law demandeth, Christ hath already endured. "It is finished!" And when ye have done this, go ye next to the benighted votaries of Rome, when ye see the priests with their backs to the people, offering every day the pretended sacrifice of the mass, and lifting up the host on high—a sacrifice, they say—"an unbloody sacrifice for the quick and the dead,"—cry, "Cease, false priest, cease! for 'it is finished!' Cease, false worshipper, cease to bow, for 'it is finished!' " God neither asks nor accepts any other sacrifice than that which Christ offered once for all upon the cross. Go ye next to the foolish among your own countrymen who call themselves Protestants, but who are Papists after all, who think by their gifts and their gold, by their prayers and their vows, by their church-goings and their chapel-goings, by their baptisms and their confirmations, to make themselves fit for God; and say to them, "Stop, 'it is finished;' God needs not this of you. He has received enough; why will ye pin your rags to the fine linen of Christ's righteousness? Why will you add your counterfeit farthing to the costly ransom which Christ has paid in to the treasure-house of God? Cease from your pains, your doings, your performances, for 'it is finished;' Christ has done it all." This one text is enough to blow the Vatican to the four winds. Lay but this beneath Popery, and like a train of gunpowder beneath a rock, it shall blast it into the air. This is a thunderclap against all human righteousness. Only let this come like a two-edged sword, and your good works and your fine performances are soon cast away. "It is finished." Why improve on what is finished? Why add to that which is complete? The Bible is finished, he that adds to it shall have his name taken out of the Book of Life, and out of the holy city: Christ's atonement is finished, and he that adds to that must expect the selfsame doom. And when ye shall have told it thus to the ears of men of every nation and of every tribe, tell it to all poor despairing souls. Ye find them on their knees, crying, "O God, what can I do to make recompense for my offences?" Tell them, "It is finished;" the recompense is made already. "O God!" they say, "how can I ever get a righteousness in which thou canst accept such a worm as I am?" Tell them, "It is finished;" their righteousness is wrought out already; they have no need to trouble themselves about adding to it, if "it is finished." Go to the poor despairing wretch, who has given himself up, not for death merely, but for damnation—he who says, "I cannot escape from sin, and I cannot be saved from its punishment." Say to him, "Sinner, the way of salvation is finished once for all." And if ye meet some professed Christians in doubts and fears, tell them, "It is finished." Why, we have hundreds and thousands that really are converted, who do not know that "it is finished." They never know that they are safe. They do not know that "it is finished." They think they have faith to-day, but perhaps they may become unbelieving to-morrow. They do not know that "it is finished." They hope God will accept them, if they do some things, forgetting that the way of acceptance is finished. God as much accepts a sinner who only believed in Christ five minutes ago, as he will a saint who has known and loved him eighty years, for he does not accept men because of any anything they do or feel, but simply and only for what Christ did, and that is finished. Oh! poor hearts! some of you do love the Saviour in a measure, but blindly. You are thinking that you must be this, and attain to that, and then you may be assured that you are saved. Oh! you may be assured of it to-day—if you believe in Christ you are saved. "But I feel imperfections."

Yes, but what of that? God does not regard your imperfections, but he covers them with Christ's righteousness. He sees them to remove them, but not to lay them to thy charge. "Ay, but I cannot be what I would be." But what if thou canst not? Yet God does not look at thee, as what thou art in thyself, but as what thou art in Christ.

Come with me, poor soul, and thou and I will stand together this morning, while the tempest gathers, for we are not afraid. How sharp that lightning flash! but yet we tremble not. How terrible that peal of thunder! and yet we are not alarmed, and why? Is there anything in us why we should escape? No, but we are standing beneath the cross—that precious cross, which like some noble lightning-conductor in the storm, takes itself all the death from the lightning, and all the fury from the tempest. We are safe. Loud mayest thou roar, O thundering law, and terribly mayest thou flash, O avenging justice! We can look up with calm delight to all the tumult of the elements, for we are safe beneath the cross.

Come with me again. There is a royal banquet spread; the King himself sits at the table, and angels are the servitors. Let us enter. And we do enter, and we sit down and eat and drink; but how dare we do this? our righteousness are as filthy rags—how could we venture to come here? Oh, because the filthy rags are not ours any longer. We have renounced our own righteousness, and therefore we have renounced the filthy rags, and now to-day we wear the royal garments of the Saviour, and are from head to foot arrayed in white, without spot or wrinkle or any such thing; standing in the clear sunlight—black, but comely; loathsome in ourselves, but glorious in him; condemned in Adam, but accepted in the Beloved. We are neither afraid nor ashamed to be with the angels of God, to talk with the glorified; nay, nor even alarmed to speak with God himself and call him our friend.

And now last of all, I publish this to sinners. I know not where thou art this morning, but may God find thee out; thou who hast been a drunkard, swearer, thief; thou who hast been a blackguard of the blackest kind; thou who hast dived into the very kennel, and rolled thyself in the mire—if to-day thou feelest that sin is hateful to thee, believe in Him who has said, "It is finished." Let me link thy hand in mine; let us come together, both of us, and say, "Here are two poor naked souls, good Lord; we cannot clothe ourselves;" and he will give us a robe, for "it is finished." "But, Lord, is it long enough for such sinners, and broad enough for such offenders?" "Yes," saith he, "it is finished." "But we need washing, Lord! Is there anything that can take away black spots so hideous as ours?" "Yes," saith he, "here is the bath of blood." "But must we not add our tears to it?" "No," says he, "no, it is finished, there is enough." "And now, Lord, thou hast washed us, and thou hast clothed us, but we would be still completely clean within, so that we may never sin any more; Lord, is there a way by which this can be done?" "Yes," saith he, "there is the bath of water which floweth from the wounded side of Christ." "And, Lord, is there enough there to wash away my guiltiness as well as my guilt?" "Ay," saith he, "it is finished." "Jesus Christ is made, unto you sanctification as well as redemption." Child of God, wilt thou have Christ's finished righteousness this morning, and wilt thou rejoice in it more than ever thou hast done before? And oh! poor sinner, wilt thou have Christ or no? "Ah," saith one, "I am willing enough, but I am not worthy." He does not want any worthiness. All he asks is willingness, for you know how he puts it, "Whoever will let him come." If he has given you willingness, you may believe in Christ's finished work this morning. "Ah!" say you, "but you cannot mean me." But I do, for it says, "Ho, every one that thirsteth." Do you thirst for Christ? Do you wish to be saved by him? "Every one that thirsteth,"—not only that young woman yonder, not simply that grey-headed old rebel yonder who has long despised the Saviour, but this mass below, and you in these double tiers of gallery—"Every one that thirsteth, come ye to the waters, and he that hath no money come." O that I could "compel" you to come! Great God, do thou make the sinner willing to be saved, for he wills to be damned, and will not come unless thou change his will! Eternal Spirit, source of light, and life, and grace, come down and bring the strangers home! "It is finished." Sinner, there is nothing for God to do. "It is finished;" there is nothing for you to do. "It is finished;" Christ need not bleed. "It is finished;" you need not weep. "It is finished;" God the Holy Spirit need not tarry because of your unworthiness, nor need you tarry because of your helplessness. "It is finished;" every stumbling-block is rolled out of the road; every gate is opened; the bars of brass are broken, the gates of iron are burst asunder. "It is finished;" come and welcome, come and welcome! The table is laid; the fatlings are killed; the oxen are ready. Lo! here stands the messenger! Come from the highways and from the hedges; come from the dens and from the kens of London; come, ye vilest of the vile; ye who hate yourselves to-day, come! Jesus bids you; oh! will you tarry? Oh! Spirit of God, do thou repeat the invitation, and make it an effectual call to many a heart, for Jesus' sake! Amen.

Delivered on Sunday morning, December 1, 1861.

6
OUR LORD'S LAST CRY FROM THE CROSS

"And when Jesus had cried with a loud voice, he said, Father, into thy hands I commend my spirit: and having said thus, he gave up the ghost."

—*Luke 23:46*

THESE were the dying words of our Lord Jesus Christ, "Father, into thy hands I commend my spirit." It may be instructive if I remind you that the words of Christ upon the cross were seven. Calling each of his cries, or utterances, by the title of a word, we speak of the seven last words of the Lord Jesus Christ. Let me rehearse them in your hearing. The first, when they nailed him to the cross, was, "Father, forgive them; for they know not what they do." Luke has preserved that word. Later, when one of the two thieves said to Jesus, "Lord, remember me when thou comest into thy kingdom," Jesus said to him, "Verily I say unto thee, To day shalt thou be with me in paradise." This also Luke has carefully preserved. Farther on, our Lord, in his great agony, saw his mother, with breaking heart, standing by the cross, and looking up to him with unutterable love and grief, and he said to her, "Woman, behold thy son!" and to the beloved disciple, "Behold thy mother!" and thus he provided a home for her when he himself should be gone away. This utterance has only been preserved by John.

The fourth and central word of the seven was, "Eloi, Eloi, lama sabachthani?" which is, being interpreted, "My God, my God, why hast thou forsaken me?" This was the culmination of his grief, the central point of all his agony. That most awful word that ever fell from the lips of man, expressing the quintessence of exceeding agony, is well put fourth, as though it had need of three words before it, and three words after it, as its body-guard. It tells of a good man, a son of God, the Son of God, forsaken of his God. That central word of the seven is found in Matthew and in Mark, but not in Luke or John; but the fifth word has been preserved by John; that is, "I thirst," the shortest, but not quite the sharpest of all the Master's words, though under a bodily aspect, perhaps the sharpest of them all. John has also treasured up another very precious saying of Jesus Christ on the cross, that is the wondrous word, "It is finished." This was the last word but one, "It is finished," the gathering up of all his lifework, for he had left nothing undone, no thread was left a ravelling, the whole fabric of redemption had been woven, like his garment, from the top throughout, and it was finished to perfection. After he had said, "It is finished," he uttered the last word of all, "Father, into thy hands I commend my spirit," which I have taken for a text tonight; but to which I will not come immediately.

There has been a great deal said about these seven cries from the cross by divers writers; and though I have read what many of them have written, I cannot add anything to what they have said, since they have delighted to dwell upon these seven last cries; and here the most ancient writers, of what would be called the Romish school, are not to be excelled, even by Protestants, in their intense devotion to every letter of our Saviour's dying words; and they sometimes strike out new meanings, richer and more rare than any that have occurred to the far cooler minds of modern critics, who are as a rule greatly blessed with moles' eyes, able to see where there is nothing to be seen, but never able to see when there is anything worth seeing. Modern criticism, like modern theology, if it were put in the Garden of Eden, would not see a flower. It is like the sirocco that blasts and burns, it is without either dew or unction; in fact, it is the very opposite of these precious things, and proves itself to be unblest of God, and unblessing to men.

Now concerning these seven cries from the cross, many authors have drawn from them lessons concerning seven duties. Listen. When our Lord said, "Father, forgive them," in effect, he said to us,

"Forgive your enemies." Even when they despitefully use you, and put you to terrible pain, be ready to pardon them. Be like the sandalwood tree, which perfumes the axe that fells it. Be all gentleness, and kindness, and love; and be this your prayer, "Father, forgive them."

The next duty is taken from the second cry, namely, that of penitence and faith in Christ, for he said to the dying thief, "To day shalt thou be with me in paradise." Have you, like him, confessed your sin? Have you his faith, and his prayerfulness? Then you shall be accepted even as he was. Learn, then, from the second cry, the duty of penitence and faith.

When our Lord, in the third cry, said to his mother, "Woman, behold thy son!" he taught us the duty of filial love. No Christian must ever be short of love to his mother, his father, or to any of those who are endeared to him by relationships which God has appointed for us to observe. Oh, by the dying love of Christ to his mother, let no man here unman himself by forgetting his mother! She bore you; bear her in her old age, and lovingly cherish her even to the last.

Jesus Christ's fourth cry teaches us the duty of clinging to God, and trusting in God: "My God, my God." See how, with both hands, he takes hold of him: "My God, my God, why hast thou forsaken me?" He cannot bear to be left of God; all else causes him but little pain compared with the anguish of being forsaken of his God. So learn to cling to God, to grip him with a double-handed faith; and if thou dost even think that he has forsaken thee, cry after him, and say, "Show me wherefore thou contendest with me, for I cannot bear to be without thee."

The fifth cry, "I thirst," teaches us to set a high value upon the fulfilment of God's Word. "After this, Jesus knowing that all things were now accomplished, that the scripture might be fulfilled, saith, I thirst." Take thou good heed, in all thy grief and weakness, still to preserve the Word of thy God, and to obey the precept, learn the doctrine, and delight in the promise. As thy Lord, in his great anguish said, "I thirst," because it was written that so he would speak, do thou have regard unto the Word of the Lord even in little things.

That sixth cry, "It is finished," teaches us perfect obedience. Go through with thy keeping of God's commandment; leave out no command, keep on obeying till thou canst say, "It is finished." Work thy likework, obey thy Master, suffer or serve according to his will, but rest not till thou canst say with thy Lord, "It is finished." "I have finished the work which thou gavest me to do."

And that last word, "Father, into thy hands I commend my spirit," teaches us resignation. Yield all things, yield up even thy spirit to God at his bidding. Stand still, and make a full surrender to the Lord, and let this be thy watchword from the first even to the last, "Into thy hands, my Father, I commend my spirit."

I think that this study of Christ's last words should interest you; therefore let me linger a little longer upon it. Those seven cries from the cross also teach us something about the attributes and offices of our Master. They are seven windows of agate, and gates of carbuncle, through which you may see him, and approach him.

First, would you see him as Intercessor? Then he cries, "Father, forgive them; for they know not what they do." Would you look at him as King? Then hear his second word, "Verily I say unto thee, To day shalt thou be with me in paradise." Would you mark him as a tender Guardian? Hear him say to Mary, "Woman, behold thy son!" and to John, "Behold thy mother!" Would you peer into the dark abyss of the agonies of his soul? Hear him cry, "My God, my God, why hast thou forsaken me?" Would you understand the reality and the intensity of his bodily sufferings? Then hear him say, "I thirst," for there is something exquisite in the torture of thirst when brought on by the fever of bleeding wounds. Men on the battle-field, who have lost much blood, are devoured with thirst, and tell you that it is the worst pang of all. "I thirst," says Jesus. See the Sufferer in the body, and understand how he can sympathize with you who suffer, since he suffered so much on the cross. Would you see him as the Finisher of your salvation? Then hear his cry, "Consummatum est"—"It is finished." Oh, glorious note! Here you see the blessed Finisher of your faith. And would you then take one more gaze, and understand how voluntary was his suffering? Then hear him say, not as one who is robbed of life, but as one who takes his soul, and hands it over to the keeping of another, "Father, into thy hands I commend my spirit."

Is there not much to be learnt from these cries from the cross? Surely these seven notes make a wondrous scale of music if we do but know how to listen to them. Let me run up the scale again. Here, first, you have Christ's fellowship with men: "Father, forgive them." He stands side by side with sinners, and tries to make an apology for them: "They know not what they do." Here is, next, his kingly power. He sets open heaven's gate to the dying thief, and bids him enter. "To day shalt thou be with me in paradise." Thirdly, behold his human relationship. How near of kin he is to us! "Woman, behold thy son!" Remember how he says, "Whosoever shall do the will of my Father who is in heaven, the same is my brother, and sister, and mother." He is bone of our bone, and flesh of our flesh. He belongs to the human family. He is more of a man than any man. As surely as he is very God of very God, he is also very man of very man, taking into himself the nature, not of the Jew only, but of the Gentile, too. Belonging to his own nationality, but rising above all, he is the Man of men, the Son of man.

See, next, his taking our sin. You say, "Which note is that?" Well, they are all to that effect; but this one chiefly, "My God, my God, why hast thou forsaken me?" It was because he bore our sins in his own body on the tree that he was forsaken of God. "He hath made him to be sin for us who knew no sin," and hence the bitter cry, "Eloi, Eloi, lama sabachthani?" Behold him, in that fifth cry, "I thirst," taking, not only our sin, but also our infirmity, and all the suffering of our bodily nature. Then, if you would see his fulness as well as his weakness, if you would see his all-sufficiency as well as his sorrow, hear him cry, "It is finished." What a wonderful fulness there is in that note! Redemption is all accomplished; it is all complete; it is all perfect. There is nothing left, not a drop of bitterness in the cup of gall; Jesus has drained it dry. There is not a farthing to be added to the ransom price; Jesus has paid it all. Behold his fulness in the cry, "It is finished." And then, if you would see how he has reconciled us to himself, behold him, the Man who was made a curse for us, returning with a blessing to his Father, and taking us with him, as he draws us all up by that last dear word, "Father, into thy hands I commend my spirit."

"Now both the Surety and sinner are free."

Christ goes back to the Father, for "It is finished," and you and I come to the Father through his perfect work.

I have only practised two or three tunes that can be played upon this harp, but it is a wonderful instrument. If it be not a harp of ten strings, it is, at any rate, an instrument of seven strings, and neither time nor eternity shall ever be able to fetch all the music out of them. Those seven dying words of the ever-living Christ will make melody for us in glory through all the ages of eternity.

I shall now ask your attention for a little time to the text itself: "Father, into thy hands I commend my spirit."

Do you see our Lord? He is dying; and as yet, his face is toward man. His last word to man is the cry, "It is finished." Hear, all ye sons of men, he speaks to you, "It is finished." Could you have a choicer word with which he should say "Adieu" to you in the hour of death? He tells you not to fear that his work is imperfect, not to tremble lest it should prove insufficient. He speaks to you, and declares with his dying utterance, "It is finished." Now he has done with you, and he turns his face the other way. His day's work is done, his more than Herculean toil is accomplished, and the great Champion is going back to his Father's throne, and he speaks; but not to you. His last word is addressed to his Father, "Father, into thy hands I commend my spirit." These are his first words in going home to his Father, as "It is finished," is his last word as, for a while, he quits our company. Think of these words, and may they be your first words, too, when you return to your Father! May you speak thus to your Divine Father in the hour of death! The words were much hackneyed in Romish times; but they are not spoilt even for that. They used to be said in the Latin by dying men, "In manus tuas, Domine, commendo spiritum meum." Every dying man used to try to say those words in Latin; and if he did not, somebody tried to say them for him. They were made into a kind of spell of witchcraft; and so they lost that sweetness to our ears in the Latin; but in the English they shall always stand as the very essence of music for a dying saint, "Father, into thy hands I commend my spirit."

It is very noteworthy that the last words that our Lord used were quoted from the Scriptures. This sentence is taken, as I daresay most of you know, from the thirty-first Psalm, and the fifth verse. Let me read it to you. What a proof it is of how full Christ was of the Bible! He was not one of those who think little of the Word of God. He was saturated with it. He was as full of Scripture as the fleece of Gideon was full of dew. He could not speak even in his death without uttering Scripture. This is how David put it, "Into thine hand I commit my spirit: thou hast redeemed me, O Lord God of truth." Now, beloved, the Saviour altered this passage, or else it would not quite have suited him. Do you see, first, he was obliged, in order to fit it to his own case, to add something to it? What did he add to it? Why, that word, "Father." David said, "Into thine hand I commit my spirit;" but Jesus says, "Father, into thy hands I commend my spirit." Blessed advance! He knew more than David did, for he was more the Son of God than David could be. He was the Son of God in a very high and special sense by eternal filiation; and so he begins the prayer with, "Father." But then he takes something from it. It was needful that he should do so, for David said, "Into thine hand I commit my spirit: thou hast redeemed me." Our blessed Master was not redeemed, for he was the Redeemer; and he could have said, "Into thine hand I commit my spirit, for I have redeemed my people;" but that he did not choose to say. He simply took that part which suited himself, and used it as his own, "Father, into thy hands I commend my spirit." Oh, my brethren, you will not do better, after all, than to quote Scripture, especially in prayer. There are no prayers so good as those that are full of the Word of God. May all our speech be flavoured with texts! I wish that it were more so. They laughed at our Puritan forefathers because the very names of their children were fetched out of passages of Scripture; but I, for my part, had much rather be laughed at for talking much of Scripture than for talking much of trashy novels—novels with which (I am ashamed to say it) many a sermon nowadays is larded, ay, larded with novels that are not fit for decent men to read, and which are coated over till one hardly knows whether he is hearing about a historical event, or only a piece of fiction—from which abomination, good Lord, deliver us!

So, then, you see how well the Saviour used Scripture, and how, from his first battle with the devil in the wilderness till his last struggle with death on the cross, his weapon was ever, "It is written."

Now, I am coming to the text itself, and I am going to preach from it for only a very short time. In doing so, firstly, let us learn the doctrine of this last cry from the cross; secondly, let us practise the duty; and thirdly, let us enjoy the privilege.

I. First, LET US LEARN THE DOCTRINE of our Lord's last cry from the cross.

What is the doctrine of this last word of our Lord Jesus Christ? God is his Father, and God is our Father. He who himself said, "Father," did not say for himself, "Our Father," for the Father is Christ's Father in a higher sense than he is ours; but yet he is not more truly the Father of Christ than he is our Father if we have believed in Jesus. "Ye are all the children of God by faith in Christ Jesus." Jesus said to Mary Magdalene, "I ascend unto my Father, and your Father; and to my God, and your God." Believe the doctrine of the Fatherhood of God to his people. As I have warned you before, abhor the doctrine of the universal fatherhood of God, for it is a lie, and a deep deception. It stabs at the heart, first, of the doctrine of the adoption, which is taught in Scripture, for how can God adopt men if they are all his children already? In the second place, it stabs at the heart of the doctrine of regeneration, which is certainly taught in the Word of God. Now it is by regeneration and faith that we become the children of God, but how can that be if we are the children of God already? "As many as received him, to them gave he power to become the sons of God, even to them that believe on his name: which were born, not of blood, nor of the will of the flesh, nor of the will of man, but of God." How can God give to men the power to become his sons if they have it already? Believe not that lie of the devil, but believe this truth of God, that Christ and all who are by living faith in Christ may rejoice in the Fatherhood of God.

Next learn this doctrine, that in this fact lies our chief comfort. In our hour of trouble, in our time of warfare, let us say, "Father." You notice that the first cry from the cross is like the last; the highest note is like the lowest. Jesus begins with, "Father, forgive them," and he finishes with, "Father, into thy hands I commend my spirit." To help you in a stern duty like forgiveness, cry, "Father." To help you in sore suffering and death, cry, "Father." Your main strength lies in your being truly a child of God.

Learn the next doctrine, that dying is going home to our Father. I said to an old friend, not long ago, "Old Mr. So-and-so has gone home." I meant that he was dead. He said, "Yes, where else should he go?" I thought that was a wise question. Where else should we go? When we grow grey, and our day's work is done, where should we go but home? So, when Christ has said, "It is finished," his next word, of course, is "Father." He has finished his earthly course, and now he will go home to heaven. Just as a child runs to its mother's bosom when it is tired, and wants to fall asleep, so Christ says, "Father," ere he falls asleep in death.

Learn another doctrine, that if God is our Father, and we regard ourselves as going home when we die, because we go to him, then he will receive us. There is no hint that we can commit our spirit to God, and yet that God will not have us. Remember how Stephen, beneath a shower of stones, cried, "Lord Jesus, receive my spirit." Let us, however we may die, make this our last emotion if not our last expression, "Father, receive my spirit." Shall not our heavenly Father receive his children? If ye, being evil, receive your children at nightfall, when they come home to sleep, shall not your Father, who is in heaven, receive you when your day's work is done? That is the doctrine we are to learn from this last cry from the cross, the Fatherhood of God and all that comes of it to believers.

II. Secondly, LET US PRACTISE THE DUTY.

That duty seems to me to be, first, resignation. Whenever anything distresses and alarms you, resign yourself to God. Say, "Father, into thy hands I commend my spirit." Sing with Faber,—

> "I bow me to thy will, O God,
>   And all thy ways adore;
> And every day I live I'll seek
>   To please thee more and more."

Learn, next, the duty of prayer. When thou art in the very anguish of pain, when thou art surrounded by bitter griefs of mind as well as of body, still pray. Drop not the "Our Father." Let not your cries be addressed to the air; let not your moans be to your physician, or your nurse; but cry, "Father." Does not a child so cry when it has lost its way? If it be in the dark at night, and it starts up in a lone room, does it not cry out, "Father"; and is not a father's heart touched by that cry? Is there anybody here who has never cried to God? Is there one here who has never said "Father"? Then, my Father, put thy love into their hearts, and make them to-night say, "I will arise, and go to my Father." You shall truly be known to be the sons of God if that cry is in your heart and on your lips.

The next duty is the committal of ourselves to God by faith. Give yourselves up to God, trust yourselves with God. Every morning, when you get up, take yourself, and put yourself into God's custody; lock yourself up, as it were, in the casket of divine protection; and every night, when you have unlocked the box, ere you fall asleep, lock it again, and give the key into the hand of him who is able to keep you when the image of death is on your face. Before you sleep, commit yourself to God; I mean, do that when there is nothing to frighten you, when everything is going smoothly, when the wind blows softly from the south, and the barque is speeding towards its desired haven, still make not thyself quiet with thine own quieting. He who carves for himself will cut his fingers, and get an empty plate. He who leaves God to carve for him shall often have fat things full of marrow placed before him. If thou canst trust, God will reward thy trusting in a way that thou knowest not as yet.

And then practise one other duty, that of the personal and continual realization of God's presence. "Father, into thy hands I commend my spirit." "Thou art here; I know that thou art. I realize that thou art here in the time of sorrow, and of danger; and I put myself into thy hands. Just as I would give myself to the protection of a policeman, or a soldier, if anyone attacked me, so do I commit myself to thee, thou unseen Guardian of the night, thou unwearied Keeper of the day. Thou shalt cover my head in the day of battle. Beneath thy wings will I trust, as a chick hides beneath the hen."

See, then, your duty. It is to resign yourself to God, pray to God, commit yourself to God, and rest in a sense of the presence of God. May the Spirit of God help you in the practice of such priceless duties as these!

III. Now, lastly, LET US ENJOY THE PRIVILEGE.

First, let us enjoy the high privilege of resting in God in all times of danger and pain. The doctor has just told you that you will have to undergo an operation. Say, "Father, into thy hands I commend my spirit."

There is every probability that that weakness of yours, or that disease of yours, will increase upon you, and that by-and-by you will have to take to your bed, and lie there perhaps for many a day. Then say, "Father, into thy hands I commend my spirit." Do not fret; for that will not help you. Do not fear the future; for that will not aid you. Give yourself up (it is your privilege to do so) to the keeping of those dear hands that were pierced for you, to the love of that dear heart which was set abroach with the spear to purchase your redemption. It is wonderful what rest of spirit God can give to a man or a woman in the very worst condition. Oh, how some of the martyrs have sung at the stake! How they have rejoiced when on the rack! Bonner's coal-hole, across the water there, at Fulham, where he shut up the martyrs, was a wretched place to lie in on a cold winter's night; but they said, "They did rouse them in the straw, as they lay in the coal-hole; with the sweetest singing out of heaven, and when Bonner said, 'Fie on them that they should make such a noise!' they told him that he, too, would make such a noise if he was as happy as they were." When you have commended your spirit to God, then you have sweet rest in time of danger and pain.

The next privilege is that of a brave confidence, in the time of death, or in the fear of death. I was led to think over this text by using it a great many times last Thursday night. Perhaps none of you will ever forget last Thursday night. I do not think that I ever shall, if I live to be as old as Methuselah. From this place till I reached my home, it seemed one continued sheet of fire; and the further I went, the more vivid became the lightning flashes; but when I came at last to turn up Leigham Court Road, then the lightning seemed to come in very bars from the sky; and at last, as I reached the top of the hill, and a crash came of the most startling kind, down poured a torrent of hail, hailstones that I will not attempt to describe, for you might think that I exaggerated, and then I felt, and my friend with me, that we could hardly expect to reach home alive. We were there at the very centre and summit of the storm. All around us, on every side, and all within us, as it were, seemed nothing but the electric fluid; and God's right arm seemed bared for war. I felt then, "Well, now I am very likely going home," and I commended my spirit to God; and from that moment, though I cannot say that I took much pleasure in the peals of thunder, and the flashes of lightning, yet I felt quite as calm as I do here at this present moment; perhaps a little more calm than I do in the presence of so many people; happy at the thought that, within a single moment, I might understand more than all I could ever learn on earth, and see in an instant more than I could hope to see if I lived here for a century. I could only say to my friend, "Let us commit ourselves to God; we know that we are doing our duty in going on as we are going, and all is well with us." So we could only rejoice together in the prospect of being soon with God. We were not taken home in the chariot of fire; we are still spared a little longer to go on with life's work; but I realize the sweetness of being able to have done with it all, to have no wish, no will, no word, scarcely a prayer, but just to take one's heart up, and hand it over to the great Keeper, saying, "Father, take care of me. So let me live, so let me die. I have henceforth no desire about anything; let it be as thou pleasest. Into thy hands I commend my spirit."

This privilege is not only that of having rest in danger, and confidence in the prospect of death; it is also full of consummate joy. Beloved, if we know how to commit ourselves into the hands of God, what a place it is for us to be in! What a place to be in,—in the hands of God! There are the myriads of stars; there is the universe itself; God's hand upholds its everlasting pillars, and they do not fall. If we get into the hands of God, we get where all things rest, and we get home and happiness. We have got out of the nothingness of the creature into the all-sufficiency of the Creator. Oh, get you there; hasten to get you there, beloved friends, and live henceforth in the hands of God!

"It is finished." You have not finished; but Christ has. It is all done. What you have to do will only be to work out what he has already finished for you, and show it to the sons of men in your lives. And because it is all finished, therefore say, "Now, Father, I return to thee. My life henceforth shall be to be in thee. My joy shall be to shrink to nothing in the presence of the All-in-all, to die into the eternal life, to sink my ego into Jehovah, to let my manhood, my creaturehood live only for its Creator, and manifest only the Creator's glory. O beloved, begin to-morrow morning and end to-night with, "Father, into thy hands I commend my spirit." The Lord be with you all! Oh, if you have never prayed, God help you to begin to pray now, for Jesus' sake! Amen.

Delivered on Lord's-day Evening, June 9th, 1889.

ABOUT THE AUTHOR

Charles Haddon Spurgeon, known as "The Prince of Preachers", was a famous Reformed Baptist preacher born in Essex, England in 1834. A full-time preacher by the age of 17, Spurgeon preached an estimated 3,600 sermons by the time of his death in 1892. Spurgeon frequently preached to audiences larger than 10,000, while his printed sermons reached tens of thousands more each week.

Spurgeon authored almost 50 volumes including the classic works *All of Grace, Morning & Evening, Encouraged to Pray, Lectures to My Students,* and *The Treasury of David: A Commentary on the Psalms*. More than a century after his death, Spurgeon's devotional writings continue to touch hearts around the world. Once when asked the secret of his success, Spurgeon replied, "My people pray for me."

MINISTRIES WE LOVE

Cross-Points Books loves organizations committed to building Christ's church by proclaiming the gospel, resourcing leaders, and training workers for the harvest. Here are some of our favorite ministries:

9Marks — Building Healthy Churches (www.9marks.org)

Desiring God — Helping people understand and embrace the truth that God is most glorified in us when we are most satisfied in him. (www.desiringgod.org)

Matthias Media — An evangelical publisher of gospel-centered resources. (www.matthiasmedia.com)

Leadership Resources — A global ministry training pastors in 30+ countries to preach expository sermons, train other expositors, and foster movements of God's Word. (www.leadershipresources.org)

The Gospel Coalition — Encouraging and educating Christian leaders by advocating gospel-centered principles and practices that glorify the Savior and do good to those for whom he shed his life's blood. (www.thegospelcoalition.org)

The Spurgeon Center — Making visible the life, legacy, and library of Charles Haddon Spurgeon. (center.spurgeon.org)

Unlocking the Bible — Delivering the gospel through modern media. The teaching ministry of Colin S. Smith. (www.unlockingthebible.org)

CONNECT WITH CROSS-POINTS

For news on upcoming releases and deals on resources
promoting sound doctrine and godly devotion,
visit Cross-Points.org or follow us on social media.

Made in the USA
Las Vegas, NV
02 April 2024